THE REALLY GOOD NEWS ABOUT GOD

Barry Tattersall

Geelong, Victoria, Australia
www.ibtechservices.com.au

The Really Good News About God
Copyright © 2015 by IBTECH Services
All rights reserved.

Any passage, except quotes from other sources, may be reproduced in any form whatsoever without permission from the author. However, the author asserts the moral right to be identified as the author of this work.

ISBN: 978-0-9942627-3-8 (Paperback Version)
ISBN: 978-0-9942627-0-7 (EPUB version)
ISBN: 978-0-9942627-1-4 (MOBI version)

Scripture quotations marked [NIV] are taken from The Holy Bible, New International Version. Copyright © 1973, 1978, 1984, 2011 by Biblica Inc. Used by permission. All rights reserved.

Scripture quotations marked [GNT] are from the Good News Translation in Today's English Version- Second Edition Copyright © 1992 by American Bible Society. Used by Permission.

Scripture quotations marked [CEV] are from the Contemporary English Version. Copyright © 1991, 1992, 1995 by American Bible Society. Used by Permission.

Scripture quotations marked [Phillips] are from The New Testament in Modern English. Copyright © 1958, 1960, 1972 by J.B.Phillips. Used by Permission.

Scripture quotations marked [TM] are taken from The Message. Copyright © 1993, 1994, 1995, 1996, 2000, 2001, 2002.
Used by permission of NavPress Publishing Group.

Scripture quotations marked [BV] are not copyrighted — see Appendix.

Acknowledgements

I have been exploring and teaching the major themes of the Bible for decades. In that time I have studied the writings of dozens of authors and have held extended discussions with significant others as I have striven to understand the truths God has, and is, revealing to humankind.

As a result, the thinking and currently-held beliefs that are addressed in this short volume have been influenced by many people — far too many to remember and personally acknowledge here. Indeed some might not want to be acknowledged here, as their contribution to my thinking was counter to the theme of the book and therefore provided very helpful testing and refining of my text.

So this book is hardly a solo production.
It is the product of my personal study and research, together with the learning from these others.
This osmosis process has occurred over so many years than I am unable to be sure from where any particular thought or storyline or one-liner might have come.
In a similar vein, I have collected pictures and line drawings over the years, especially from the internet, and have no idea where most of them came from. I have taken the liberty of using a few of them here, hoping they are in the public domain or are generous offerings to the wider web world.

So if you see something here that you feel is yours, and for which I should have given credit, please accept my apology.
If you get in touch with me about it, I will acknowledge the source on the book's website and in future editions.

Having said that, I am well aware of the recent contributions made by several fellow-travellers to the end product which is now presented.

To my blogger and reviewer groups from Queensland and Victoria, to my editor from the United States, and to my grandchildren who have played with cover designs and photographs, a hearty and sincere thank you.

My major acknowledgement is to God's precious gift to me, my wonderful wife, Isabel.
For decades she has joined me and supported me in the projects God has allocated, and in which she has laboured and sacrificed much, often without appropriate appreciation and credit, and always without the time and support that should have been given her by a loving and appreciative husband.

So when I retired, I tried to make it up to her.
She was to be my next "project".
The next "era" of my life was to spend quality time with her and to give her the attention and companionship that our previous projects regularly took from her.

However, she has again been short-changed.
She has made the sacrifice that families of all authors make, to endure long hours alone in the next room while lovingly supporting and encouraging me as I, and my helpers, have brought this project to reality.
Thank you, again, my dear wife and best friend. I never cease to thank God for you.

Finally, thank you Jesus for your life, death and resurrection, which make our lives purposeful and complete, and for your promise to make all things new, which inspires us to join you in the journey towards that glorious future.

Barry Tattersall
January, 2015

Table of Contents

	Foreword	vii
	Preface	xi
	Introduction - Challenging the Status Quo	15
	Prologue - The Grand Stage Production	27
1.	God's Unconditional, Unfailing Love	33
2.	God's Supreme Sovereignty	63
3.	God's Awesome Plan	97
4.	God's Champion Lifesaver	119
5.	God's Merciful Judgement	143
6.	God — The Perfect Parent	173
7.	Our On-Stage Role	191
	Appendix - The Bible and How it is Used Here	209

Foreword

I've often thought that the Reformation did not begin and end with Martin Luther. In my view of Church history, the real message in Scripture has been finding clarification in greater measure with every century since the Dark Ages.

So many concepts we take for granted today, such as the forgiveness of sins, as just one example, were not necessarily clear 200 years ago. This too would depend on the denomination one had exposure to. Some denominations change and learn more slowly than others — some don't change or keep learning at all!

I don't need to propose here that Barry Tattersall is a great reformer. I can leave that up to the reader to decide, and perhaps time as well. Most concepts, if new, are not easily digested. This is certainly true in church settings. The warnings against false teaching are valid. Still, not every new concept is a false teaching, as history has proven. They just tend to meet resistance.

It must have been just prior to the GFC, when I first met Barry, some 8 years or so ago. A friend and pastor of mine suggested I get to meet Barry. My friend had met Barry somewhere, and thinking Barry and I lived in the same suburb of Brisbane, I should meet him, as I was just starting a house church in our suburb.

My friend had no idea what he was unleashing into my life. Neither did I when I first called Barry. There is always that sense of the unknown when you introduce yourself to a complete stranger over the phone. I did tell Barry though that I felt the Holy Spirit wanted me to meet him, and that was good enough for Barry. I'm glad it was.

I don't know how it came up, but in our first meeting, over tea in my living room, we got onto the subject of hell fire and how strange it would be for a God of love to burn people for eternity.

I'd already figured that that concept was absurd. I'd settled on the concept that unrepentant sinners would simply be snuffed out in hell fire as it was far more merciful. I had no idea that there was another way of looking at the subject.

Barry already knew that people could be really hard to budge from ingrained thinking. Still, he must have thought it was at least worth sharing with me what he had been studying.

He blew me away!

I'd never heard anyone expound on the Scriptures to show that God had a plan of salvation for everyone he loved, and not just a few. I didn't swallow it hook, line, and sinker straight away. I needed time to think. It was radical. It was something I'd never heard before. Nevertheless, I couldn't refute anything he said.

Barry and I agreed that our first meeting would not be the last. There was a lot more to talk about.

I remember asking God in prayer after Barry was gone if the Good News really was better than I had previously thought. Was it really Good News, and Good News for everyone?

I was in total awe at the thought of it. Could the Gospel message really be this good?

Over time I had to conclude that it was. It really was a "Good News" Gospel! How bizarre is that?

I was finally "undone".

Naturally many could not agree with me. If one has grown up with a "bad news" gospel, it can be hard to see it differently.

I also found that most people's views of God and his somewhat negative Gospel message (speaking of their Gospel version) were really just human projections of our base personalities onto the nature of God.

Barry has tried to reach beyond our human projections, and really bring into light the real nature of a God of love, and what that truly represents. The fact that he can use Scripture to do this, in spite of how often man has misquoted it (in my view anyway), is an achievement indeed.

So don't hold back. Keep reading, and find out just how really good, Good News can be!

Roger Hooper
Brisbane, Australia

Preface

As the Principal of a Christian Boarding School several decades ago, I taught a Bible Study class to students and staff every Wednesday evening.
Each second year we would study the Book of Revelation, as eschatology (the study of last things or end times) had become an urgent interest to many Christians as the year 2000 began to loom on the not-too-distant horizon.

I am not sure we fully or even correctly answered many of the great questions that were being asked at that time, but we had lots of lively discussion and learnt so much about the Bible and its major themes.

My sons were students in those classes and one of them, who continued to live close to us after he married and began his own family, asked if I could find my old "Revelation notes" as he wanted to study the subject again.
We decided instead to start a fresh study together one evening a week and invited a few others we knew would be interested.

In those studies we raised some very profound questions about the end times destination of various groups of people.
One of these was, "What happens to those who have never heard about Jesus?"

Although this was raised within the context of our "end times" studies, it soon took on a life of its own.
So it wasn't long before we digressed into a full study of God's plan of salvation, putting "end times" on the back-burner for a while.

In my much younger years, I had been taught that all unbelievers in Jesus Christ, regardless of why they were so, would go to a place called hell to be tormented forever.

This seemed grossly unfair to me, but we had somehow overlooked that ethical concern to remain "true to the faith".
It seemed even more strange that this outcome of endless torment was said to be under the supervision of a God of unconditional and unfailing love.

We agreed that something was terribly wrong with what I had been taught — about the future, about God, or about both.

This was the stimulus that changed our Bible study topic from eschatology to God's plan of salvation (soteriology, if you'll excuse a big theological word for it).
That study has grown in intensity for me, and has consumed me, over the last decade or two.

When we began it, we thought we were in uncharted waters as we began to stumble upon the answers I will share in this book.
Now it seems there are many people in the world and over the centuries, especially in the first 400 or 500 years of church history, and also in its last 200 years, who have made similar discoveries and come to similar conclusions as I have now done.

The study is not finished; it never will be.
I still have much to discover about God's heart and his intentions, and especially his ways of achieving them.

I therefore make no claim to infallibility.
If you've heard my views over the years, you will know that my understanding of God, his plans and his methods, has grown and therefore changed over time.
I am hopeful that this process will continue right up until the day I leave this planet.

But it is now time to write and share my current understandings about God and his plans to save the world.

If you have had no previous contact with the Christian faith, I hope you will find this a refreshing and exciting read.

If you have some background in a Christian church, of whatever variety, I invite you to read and consider what I have written with an open Bible and an open mind like a true Berean (Acts 17:11), as the ideas here will probably challenge some of your current thinking. They certainly challenged (and changed) mine.

INTRODUCTION

Challenging the Status Quo

THIS is a book I just had to write.
I have been a Christian for about 60 years.
I have also been a part of the institutional church, the most visible expression of mainstream Christianity, for many of those years.
I have supported that church, preached its doctrines, helped administer its programs and served it in many other ways.
So, I know the institutional church pretty well and have done my best to help it achieve the purpose Jesus Christ had in mind when he established his church.

The organised church has its good and not so good points.
It can be a great place to worship God — as can a beach or a rainforest.
It can be a great place to hang out with friends who love God as you do — as can a local park or coffee shop.

It can be a great place to study the Bible with fellow travellers — as can a nice warm lounge room on a winter's night.

What it does best is what can best be done in a structured or organised fashion with larger groups of people — things like corporate worship, and large scale mission and community projects.

Nevertheless, I must add, if we as individuals and families, and as small groups of individuals and families, took the instructions of Jesus seriously and shared the good news he gave us and met the physical and social needs of our local neighbourhoods, there would be fewer projects needing the larger numbers or large scale organisation the institutional church provides.

On and off, and particularly in more recent times, I have become discouraged by some aspects of the institutional church.
This is especially true of a few of its most widely known beliefs or doctrines.

Although there is a large variety of beliefs and practices within the Christian world, there are, quite remarkably, two particular views that seem to be predominantly held (and passionately defended) with which I disagree.

The first is, that Jesus Christ, the Son of God, who came to this planet to be the Saviour of the world, will almost totally fail in his mission.
And the second is, that everyone who does not become "a believer in Jesus" in their lifetime on this planet will be sentenced to misery in a place usually called hell — and for eternity.

Put together, it can be said that mainstream Christianity, by and large, promotes a God of conditional love whose attempt to save the world at Calvary was not good enough to overcome Adam's sin for the vast majority of creation.

Although its leadership might not openly admit it, the institutional church believes that God can't or won't save the whole world, even though he originally said he wanted to.

You might already be thinking, "What's this guy on about? My church isn't like that at all!"

If your church is not like that, then congratulations, you are in a wonderful place and you probably don't need to read this book any further.
But many churches *are* like that.
If you are unsure or curious about this, please check what your church really does believe and teach ... or keep reading, just in case.

How widespread is this diluted version of the good news became very clear to me when I agreed to a four week preaching assignment in a typical protestant Christian church not so long ago while its Pastor was on annual leave.

For the underlying theme of my four sermons, I planned to use the stories of the lost sheep, the lost coin and the lost sons from Luke Chapter 15 in the New Testament of the Bible.
The four messages were to focus on the loving and forgiving father, the behaviour and fate of the two sons, suggestions for a more appropriate response from the elder brother, and the real mission and purpose of the local church.

In my first message I aimed to paint the biggest Biblical picture of God I could and to invite the congregation to paint their own biggest pictures.
I preached about the correct meaning of "prodigal" and how the father was so prodigal in his attitude and behaviour — recklessly extravagant with his love, forgiveness, grace and restoration.
I applied this to God, while pointing out that most Christians don't see God with such prodigality as these parables of Jesus portray him.

To illustrate, I briefly described Calvinism (the view that people either go to heaven or hell as a result of God's prior sovereign choice) and Arminianism (the view that people either go to heaven or hell as a result of their own free will choices), and showed how these two most common Christian views fell way short of the views of God expressed in the "lost stories" of Jesus, as recorded by Luke.

I then shared what I saw as the Biblical view of God — a God of unconditional and unfailing love and supreme sovereignty who could and would do whatever was necessary to ensure that everyone eventually returned home.
I finished by again encouraging those present to create their own biggest view of God.

The response was most interesting.
Several people clapped when I finished speaking — which is very unusual in a Sunday morning church service.
Several others came and thanked me for a message they "really needed to hear".

A couple came and asked questions because the thought that God might eventually get everyone home was new to them and they wanted to know more. A couple of others came and politely said they disagreed with the view I shared.

The elders of the church were agitated and required me to attend a meeting with them during the coming week as they said many people were upset with the idea that God might eventually get all of his prodigals home.

They also said that my message had caused division in the congregation and some of those who regularly attended were not going to return to the church until I was no longer in the pulpit to share such ideas as this.

As far as I knew, the church had no written statement of faith, and people who belonged to the church, whether as members, partners or of some other designation, were not required to subscribe to an agreed set of beliefs.
I was therefore interested to discover what rule or code I had broken to cause the key players in the church to be so upset, and was equally keen to engage in discussion with the elders over the main points of my sermon and the Biblical support for them.

At the subsequent elders' meeting, which was cordial and respectful, there seemed to be only two items on the agenda.
I was told I could not continue my preaching assignment, and, it was thought that it would be better for the congregation if I didn't even attend the church again in the remaining time I was in town.

> *The "Status Quo" seems to be the world's most protected species.*

After agreeing to abide by these directions, and since there had been no discussion up to this point of my "offending view", just that it had caused problems, I asked if we could discuss that view, or at least if I could share the Biblical basis for it.
I was politely, but cautiously, given a short time to do so.

Disappointingly, one elder, in reluctantly giving assent to my request, said that whatever I said or showed him would make no difference to his opinion on the matter.
That really shocked me!
A spiritual leader in the church would not have his opinions or views influenced by what the Bible had to say on a fundamental matter of faith.
What a sad opening statement to a study of the Scriptures by a church leadership group!

Nevertheless, I proceeded to show them what the Bible had to say on the subject.

One elder recorded the verses I shared.

Another said he would like to give those verses some further thought. The others remained fairly silent throughout.

I was asked a few questions, one of which was how this view of God and his possible success in saving the world had changed my life. Many of them seemed surprised that my answer included describing my increased motivation for sharing the good news with those who are currently unreconciled to God.

The whole episode was a sad and disappointing one.
I guess I was as surprised as I was saddened by the elders' dramatic response and the course of action they took before they had even discussed the matter with me.

I might have expected such a strong reaction if I had shared an idea that belittled God or discounted the work of Jesus on the cross in some way.
But getting that response after sharing a view that enhanced our concept of God's love and grace, and which gave Christ's work on the cross its fullest possible scope and effect, really surprised me in a Christian church, and especially in one that so openly and frequently preached on the subject of God's grace.

The idea of writing a book on the subject had always been floating around in my mind and I supposed that it might happen some day. But this incident galvanised the idea into a firm determination that a book had to be written.
If this was the stance taken by a Bible-believing, grace-motivated church ...

I felt overwhelmed by the task — not of writing the book as such, but of getting it published and read by those who might be living comfortably and unthinkingly in the land of mainstream Christianity.

Since I began writing, I have found that other Christians don't want to discuss the matter either.
It's different "from the way we've been taught", and therefore of no interest, is a common response.

The "Status Quo" seems to be the world's most protected species.

It survives every challenge society throws at it.
In particular, the institutional church over the centuries has a distinguished record in ensuring the Status Quo remains alive and well in every generation, even if there is no known reason for it to be doing so.

A wonderful story is told about five monkeys who are placed together in a large cage.
Inside the cage hangs a banana from a string, with a set of steps directly underneath.
Before long one of the monkeys approaches the steps and starts to climb towards the banana.
As soon as the monkey begins to climb, all the other monkeys are sprayed with cold water from outside the cage.

After a while a second monkey attempts to get the banana.
Again all the other monkeys are sprayed with cold water, and this routine continues for several days.
Eventually, whenever a monkey merely approaches the steps, it is attacked by the other monkeys to prevent it from climbing, even before any cold water is sprayed, because they know what the consequences will be.

At this stage, one of the monkeys is removed from the cage and replaced with a new one.
It isn't long before the new monkey sees the banana and approaches the steps.
To his complete surprise, the other monkeys attack him.

After another attempt and another attack, he decides that if he tries to climb the steps he will be assaulted, so doesn't ever try again.

Then another of the original monkeys is replaced by a newcomer, who doesn't take long to catch sight of the banana and approach the steps.
He is attacked by the other monkeys, including the previous newcomer, who has no idea why they are not permitted to climb the steps or why he has participated in the attack on the new monkey.

This process is continued until all the original monkeys have been replaced.
The cage now contains only new monkeys, none of whom has been sprayed with cold water or even knows about the cold water.
Nevertheless, no monkey ever again approaches the steps to take the banana.
Why not?
Because as far as they know, that's the way it has always been around here.
The Status Quo survives again.

> ... *the God of love who created ... our world has a loving purpose for it.*

As you read the chapters of this book, you will probably find yourself thinking "that can't be right".
Why not?
Is it because you have never thought about it that way?
If you have no better reason to reject something than say, "It has never been that way", then please resist the temptation to reject it and decide to think it through.

Take the challenge to open your Bible and your mind and discover whether your currently held position, the view you have always held, can really be backed by Scripture, or is just maintaining the Status Quo you inherited from an original monkey.

In my church story above, no-one wanted to discuss what I had said. It was just different to the way "we think about things around here", so was out-of-order.
Even what the Bible had to say on the matter seemed to be of no interest to one leader.

My aim in writing this book is two fold.
Firstly, I wish to show that the God of love who created and is in control of our world has a loving purpose for it and has the power and determination to see his purpose accomplished.
It is a most exciting story.

Most sections of mainstream Christianity preach what they call the good news.
But, in many of these, it really is a mixture of good news for a few and very bad news for the majority.
This book will show you that the Bible, read with an open mind and through the twin lenses of God's love and sovereignty, describes what the good news really is.

Secondly, I wish to offset, at least to some extent, the contribution I have made in years past to the view promoted by many churches that God's love is conditional and his attempt at salvation was insufficient to overcome Adam's sin for most of his creation.
I carelessly and unthinkingly supported, and even preached, this line during much of the time I was serving those churches.
I now want to publicly admit that I was wrong with that support and preaching, and share what I now believe is the truth of the matter.

The book has a prologue and seven chapters.
◊ Prologue — "The Grand Stage Production" — is an invitation to imagine our world as a theatrical stage production.

◊ Chapter One — "God's Unconditional, Unfailing Love" — discusses God's extravagant love as the motivating factor for all that he does.

◊ Chapter Two — "God's Supreme Sovereignty" — explores God's sovereignty — his ability to do whatever he decides and to fully achieve his purpose for his creation.

◊ Chapter Three — "God's Awesome Plan" — describes this purpose, and the plans God has to achieve it.

◊ Chapter Four — "God's Champion Lifesaver" — examines the role that Jesus Christ, God's Son, plays in achieving God's purpose.

◊ Chapter Five — "God's Merciful Judgement" — investigates judgement and punishment, and shows how God uses these in his plans for restoring the creation to its original position and condition.

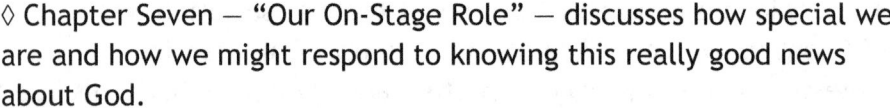

◊ Chapter Six — "God - The Perfect Parent" — uses the metaphor of a perfect parent to draw the conclusion that God really has good news for all of us.

◊ Chapter Seven — "Our On-Stage Role" — discusses how special we are and how we might respond to knowing this really good news about God.

It should be easy reading — not weighed down with theological or religious terminology.
But it might not be a super fast read, as some serious thinking mixed with old-fashioned common sense will be required along the way.

Also, a website dedicated to providing more extensive notes and references will be available in 2016 for those wanting to explore the book's contents at a deeper or more theological/philosophical level. When available, it will be found at *www.ibtechservices.com.au*.

Having said that, let me quickly add that I don't pretend to have all the answers about such profound topics.

We mere humans often ponder and debate subjects like these, sometimes for years, but have little chance of producing water-tight conclusions from our limited perspective.

As is so often the case, we need to go to a higher authority or at least to a source that has a broader perspective than we have.

The Bible is that source for me.
I go to the Bible and gather clues from there, then try to formulate answers that accommodate all those clues, and are consistent with other relevant parts of the Bible.
A tall order you are thinking?
Sure is, but it's the only reliable resource we have to tackle life's big questions.

So, although I am trying to write a popular edition or lay person's book, rather than a theological treatise, I will quote a fair bit of the Bible as the story of the good news about God unfolds.

This is not to make the way heavy going for those for whom I am particularly writing.
But is for the sake of "others" who happen upon this book, those who possibly belong to a mainstream church, or have done so in times past, and for whom the storyline of this book might sound unbelievable without making reference to what God has disclosed in the Bible.

So to my readers, please read and enjoy, and refer to as little or as much of the Bible as you feel comfortable to do.

If you prefer, just jump over the Biblical quotations — they are clearly labelled and identified.

For the "others", please resist the temptation to find fault with what I have written which accurately reflects the message of the Bible.

Only criticise if I do not, and, if you do find such an instance, please contact me via the website and show me my error.
My main aim in life is to discover the truth, so if you can help me do that, I will be most grateful.

If you wish to write to me with any questions, I will do my best to answer them or to point you in the direction of someone further along the track than I am.

Equally, any suggestions you would like to offer for improvements or corrections to what I have written will be greatly appreciated and given my full consideration for future editions.

You are also welcome to debate any points that I have made — provided the debate is respectful and gracious, and the arguments advanced are Biblical ones. (I am not interested in what this person or that pastor or such-and-such professor said or wrote, only what an accurately translated Bible has to say.)
The opportunity to take any of these options will also be given on the website.

I have really enjoyed writing this for you, so please enjoy the journey from start to finish.
It has been so exciting for me to discover that after all the inconsistent and often contradictory messages that have been preached by many of our churches over the centuries, the Bible shows that God really is a good God with a really good purpose for all of us — and that he will successfully achieve that purpose.
I hope you make that discovery too.

PROLOGUE

The Grand Stage Production

WE humans have great difficulty understanding the Creator and his ways.
I should know — I've spent many years of my life trying.

One of the most helpful ideas I have had in this pursuit is to think of the events of the world as a grand stage production called LIFE in which the playwright, God, has written the script and the director, Jesus Christ, has been given the responsibility to ensure the script is faithfully performed on the stage.

This stage play idea has obvious weaknesses if taken too far, as all illustrations and parables do, so I have only been using it tentatively and privately for my own purposes until very recently, when I discovered other authors suggesting a similar idea.

For example, C.S. Lewis in *Surprised by Joy* wrote that he thought God might project us in the same way a dramatist projects his characters, and Lewis, as a character, could no more meet God as the author, than Hamlet could meet Shakespeare.

In his journey towards awareness of a personal God, Lewis decided that if Hamlet and Shakespeare were ever to meet, it must be as a result of Shakespeare's initiative and action, as Hamlet could not initiate anything of that magnitude.

Interestingly, Lewis also conjectured that Shakespeare could make himself appear as the character called "Author" in the play, and write some dialogue between Hamlet and himself.
He then explained that the "Shakespeare" in the play would be, at the same time, both himself and one of his characters, a bit like God and Jesus Christ have been in our world.

William W Bentley, Jr. wrote a short essay called *The Simple Story of the Universe*, which was presented as a Grand Drama of five acts, with several scenes in each act.

And Thomas Heywood, an English playwright of the 17th century, once said, "The world's a theatre, the earth a stage, which God and Nature do with actors fill."

Amazingly all three of these writings came to my attention in the space of just one week, so I decided I should give my stage play idea more serious consideration than I had previously done.

So, to begin with, let's suppose that ...

God, the playwright of all playwrights, wrote the script for LIFE through which his ultimate purpose for the world, the heavens and the earth, would be accomplished.

He designed the stage and backdrops for the production, and chose the role and character of each of its actors.

God's Son, Jesus Christ, created the stage, the props and the cast. He was also given the script and the responsibility to direct the play from beginning to end.

The actors had their roles to portray and their lines to deliver, but were given the freedom to interpret those characters as they saw fit, utilising their individual personalities and acting styles.

Jesus donned an earth-suit and played cameo roles on stage in several scenes throughout the production. After the final scene of the final act, Jesus presented the whole cast to God where every actor was warmly welcomed and ushered into God's eternal back-stage party to celebrate the success of the show.

> *Jesus donned an earth-suit and played cameo roles on stage in several scenes throughout the production.*

This way of looking at things helps me in several ways.

It reminds me that God is really in control of our world — every major element in the script is predestined, or pre-determined — and so helps me to trust him no matter how things appear on the surface.

It reminds me that we really have little choice in what part we play in the grand drama of life.
Who has chosen their parents or their nationality or their birth date or their personality or the people and circumstances that invade their space, for example?

Surely, it is only the playwright who makes these decisions!

As a result, some of us are chosen to become God-worshippers or "early believers" the first time we appear on stage, some at a later time, and the remainder right towards the end, or even backstage.

It reminds me to love even the villains in our lives, as their roles have been pre-determined by God (remember Judas?) and it is not yet their time to become God-worshippers.
This, in turn, helps me to cope with the mean, bad and ugly circumstances that invade my life, whether I can see God's purpose in them right now, or not.

It reminds me that God is loving and fair, and that every actor will eventually be welcomed into God's eternal family, even if the villains have to be cleaned up a bit (removing some of their make-up) before they are presented to him.

It reminds me that God is sovereign, his script will be followed under the watchful eye of the director, and the finale he has written into that script will definitely happen, and right on cue.

It reminds me that everything we see happening in the world, and in our lives, is in some way working towards that great finale, curtain call and backstage party.

Discovering this amazing secret, that life in God's world ends up with a huge celebratory backstage party for the whole cast, has been the most exciting journey of my life so far.
I hope it becomes yours too.

Please join me as we go behind the scenes and explore some of the thinking and planning of the playwright, and take a peek at a few of the production notes scattered on his desk.

On the way through, we might even bump into the director, Jesus Christ. He still turns up in cameo roles quite often, and quite unexpectedly at times.

Let's begin by building the "spectacles" we will use for looking at these issues and guiding our thinking and discussion.

Chapter One, showing that God really loves us, will put the first lens into the frame.
Let's go do it.

CHAPTER 1

God's Unconditional, Unfailing Love

MY mother became ill and died in hospital when I was nine years old.
And I had a younger brother who was six.
My father took it upon himself to raise us boys unassisted. He remained widowed for his remaining forty plus years.

He was not a wealthy man having a mundane desk job in a large manufacturing company which paid very average wages.
We lived in a modest, three bedroom house, which he converted into two flats to try to increase his weekly disposable income.

As much as we struggled to make ends meet, and to experience a normal family life without a wife and mother, we were happy, well clothed and well fed even if the meals were always the same and nights were spent mending holes in socks and pullovers ready for the next day at school.

The key to our successful upbringing was Dad's love for us.
Although his means and his time were limited, anything he could do for us he did.
I will be forever grateful to my Dad for his love, commitment and daily sacrifices.

My wife, Isabel, also had a great Dad.
He worked in the foundry of the same company my Dad worked for.
His job was hard and dirty and he earned even less than my Dad did (I think).

When I first met him, Isabel's Mum used to drive him to and from work each day.
But times weren't always like that.
For many years he would ride a push-bike twenty kilometres or more to and from work, leaving in the dark and often returning home in the dark, especially during the winter months.

The sacrifices made, the burdens carried, and the loneliness endured were because he loved his family and took his responsibility for providing for them as the number one priority in his life.
Anything that needed to be done for his family he did.

Isabel and I have four adult sons, who also have families.
Although their circumstances are quite different work-wise and financially, there is one thing they have in common.
They love their wives and children above all else and will do anything for them because of that love.

God's Love for All

Nevertheless, even the best of fathers I know and have known can't match God, our heavenly Father.
I appreciate his resources are not limited as most of ours are, but he still has to choose to use those resources in the best interests of his creation.

And the good news is that he does.

Jesus tells us that God's loving provision is unbiased, showing no respect for the worthiness or unworthiness of the recipients.

> *But I tell you, love your enemies and pray for those who persecute you, that you may be children of your Father in heaven.*
> *He causes his sun to rise on the evil and the good, and sends rain on the righteous and the unrighteous.*
> *[Matthew 5 : 44 – 45 NIV]*

The Bible also describes God's willingness to love us at such ultimate personal cost in this way ...

> *You see, at just the right time, when we were still powerless, Christ died for the ungodly.*
> *Very rarely will anyone die for a righteous person, though for a good person someone might possibly dare to die.*
> *But God demonstrates his own love for us in this: While we were still sinners, Christ died for us.*
> *[Romans 5 : 6 – 8 NIV]*

Isn't that just amazing?

It doesn't matter whether we are sinners, evil, good, righteous or unrighteous, God still loves us and provides for our well-being.
I like to say that God's love is unconditional and unfailing.
He just can't help himself.
Love is his character, his nature.
Love comes naturally to him, and everything he does is clothed in love and motivated by love.

God doesn't wait for us to become good enough or to meet any prior qualifications in behaviour or attitude.

It was while we were his enemies, out of favour with him, that he expressed his love to us in such an amazing way.

There is a major school of thought within Christian teaching that doesn't agree.
It usually goes by the name of Calvinism or predestination.
Actually, I call it the "Dad is playing favourites" view.
Its main premise is that God is sovereign and will decide the fate of every one of his creation.

> God's love is unconditional and unfailing.
> He just can't help himself.
> Love is his character, his nature.

I don't have any problem with that premise, but when Calvinists add to this the firm belief that most of his offspring will spend eternity tormented in a horrible place they call hell, God is obviously seen as the one who decided on that outcome too.

In other words, this school of thought accuses God of deciding beforehand who is going to heaven and who is going to miss out, and no-one can do a thing about it. Ugh !!!
Fancy asking someone to worship and serve a God who creates people with the intention of torturing them or their friends forever!!

Can you imagine earthly parents deciding before any of their children are born which of them they will love and care for and which of them they will abandon?

I'd rather believe the Bible when it says that God wants everyone to be saved, come to know the truth and live in harmony with him and with each other.

Whether we acknowledge it or not, we are all God's creation or, more specifically, offspring of God's original creation, and therefore the object of his unconditional love.

God made us in his image.
So we are spirit as he is, and have been placed in physical earth-suits as was his son, Jesus Christ.
Each of us is therefore a spiritual being having an earthly experience.

Having given us earth-suits and having placed us on this planet, he provides everything we need to live out our purpose in this earthly adventure, as any loving father would.

Good Mother, Good Father

Qualities of a good father are protection and provision, and fathers most often express their love for their wife and children in these ways.

But let's not forget that we have mothers as well.
And mothers' qualities, among many others, are care, comfort and compassion.

In fact mothers beautifully and consistently demonstrate the Bible's advice about how we should be loving each other ...

> *No one should seek their own good,*
> *but the good of others.*
> *[1 Corinthians 10 : 24 NIV]*

Good mothers just spend themselves on those they love, so often to their own personal detriment.
They lay down their lives for their families whenever that is needed.
How often have we seen a mother lavish her love on an undeserving child, a child who did not seem to have a single lovable quality to an outsider looking on?
What extraordinary lengths has a mother's love.

When I talk of God being a loving father, I am referring to the qualities he has of both mothers and fathers.

Why?
Because Adam was made in God's image and from within him was formed the woman.
In the original man there was both man and woman, so within God there must also be qualities of both man and woman otherwise both man and woman could not have come from Adam.

The Bible makes an incredible claim about all this love business.
It says that God *is* love.

> *God is love.*
> *Whoever lives in love lives in God, and God in them.*
> *[1 John 4 : 16 NIV]*

It's not that he has love, or that he loves, or that he is loving.
He *is* love.
And this love, his whole character, is expressed through his protection, provision, care, comfort and compassion — his father and mother qualities.

Brennan Manning also makes a similar point in his *The Signature of Jesus*. He says,

> *"If we take all the goodness, wisdom and compassion of the best mothers and fathers who have ever lived, they would only be a faint shadow of the love and mercy in the heart of the redeeming God."*

It's hard to explain, but glimpses of God's love and mercy touch me deeply, sometimes quite emotionally.
Reading books or listening to people's stories of how God's love and grace has met them at a point of need or crisis stops me in my tracks.

I choke up and tears often tumble down my cheeks when I read of Jesus having morning devotions with Papa in Paul Young's *The Shack*, for example, as Jesus expresses his appreciation of Papa's love for Mack.

I have tried reading this novel out aloud, but can't get through any chapter without choking up and having to revert to silent reading just to keep up the pace and "good appearances".

Why is this?
As much as I try to keep control, to brace myself, when I see an example of God reaching into a person's life and circumstances with his compassionate love, an emotional caress creeps up from behind and catches me off guard every time.

God's love just pushes a touchy button inside me and changes me from a detached reader to an emotional hostage.
God's love overwhelms me; it captures me, takes me prisoner.
I cannot be unaffected by it or resist it, and I certainly can't ignore it.

God's love drew me to him when I was quite young, about 12 years old. It motivated me to swim against the tide at university; and it drove me to serve him in my adult years in several pioneering projects, often helping those who had not previously experienced much love from anyone else.

When God gets you in his sights, you are unable to escape.
Not that I ever wanted to.
I am so glad he has captured me so completely, even though that has meant some incredible sacrifices and hardships and embarrassments at times, but also moments of great joy and unexpected achievements in some of the most important arenas of life.

Prodigal Father

This extraordinary love of God is displayed in my favourite parable of Jesus, as recorded by Luke in the Bible.

We often call it the "Parable of the Prodigal Son", but I prefer to call it the "Parable of the Two Lost Sons", as the older brother was just as lost as the younger.

An even better title would be the "Parable of the Prodigal Father", as the father's love is more prodigal, more extravagant and reckless, than the spending and wastefulness of the younger son.

Here is the Bible's record of the story.

> There was once a man who had two sons. The younger one said to him, 'Father, give me my share of the property now.' So the man divided his property between his two sons.
>
> After a few days the younger son sold his part of the property and left home with the money. He went to a country far away, where he wasted his money in reckless living.
>
> He spent everything he had. Then a severe famine spread over that country, and he was left without a thing. So he went to work for one of the citizens of that country, who sent him out to his farm to take care of the pigs. He wished he could fill himself with the bean pods the pigs ate, but no one gave him anything to eat.
>
> At last he came to his senses and said, 'All my father's hired workers have more than they can eat, and here I am about to starve! I will get up and go to my father and say, "Father, I have sinned against God and against you. I am no longer fit to be called your son; treat me as one of your hired workers.' So he got up and started back to his father.
>
> He was still a long way from home when his father saw him; his heart was filled with pity, and he ran, threw his arms around his son, and kissed him.

'Father,' the son said, 'I have sinned against God and against you. I am no longer fit to be called your son.'

But the father called to his servants. 'Hurry!' he said. 'Bring the best robe and put it on him. Put a ring on his finger and shoes on his feet. Then go and get the prize calf and kill it, and let us celebrate with a feast! For this son of mine was dead, but now he is alive; he was lost, but now he has been found.' And so the feasting began.

In the meantime the older son was out in the field. On his way back, when he came close to the house, he heard the music and dancing. So he called one of the servants and asked him, 'What's going on?' 'Your brother has come back home,' the servant answered, 'and your father has killed the prize calf, because he got him back safe and sound.'

The older brother was so angry that he would not go into the house; so his father came out and begged him to come in. But he spoke back to his father, 'Look, all these years I have worked for you like a slave, and I have never disobeyed your orders. What have you given me? Not even a goat for me to have a feast with my friends! But this son of yours wasted all your property on prostitutes, and when he comes back home, you kill the prize calf for him!'

'My son,' the father answered, 'you are always here with me, and everything I have is yours. But we had to celebrate and be happy, because your brother was dead, but now he is alive; he was lost, but now he has been found.'
[Luke 15 : 11 — 32 GNT]

To help people connect with the story, preachers and authors often ask their audience to identify with one or other of the two sons and so find a personal application in the story.

My preferred application is to try to identify with the Father in his loss and hurt and humiliation and then to accept the challenge to act the way he did when I am confronted with similar challenges.

People let us down, disappoint us, take advantage of us and embarrass or humiliate us all the time, so we have a lifetime of opportunities to practise and perfect being prodigal with our love, forgiveness and grace.

O to be like the father in the parable.
We won't reach perfection in this in our lifetimes, but it's something we should aspire to.
And we will make progress in this, if we allow the Holy Spirit to teach, correct and mature us.

It didn't matter how much his sons hurt and embarrassed him, and both of them did, his love for them didn't change one little bit.
He wanted both of them to be enjoying all he could give them.

Peter's Experience

Peter, James and John formed an executive of sorts of the disciple group that closely followed Jesus when he was on earth.
As a result, they shared some very special times and ministry experiences with him.

John instinctively knew God's love for him — he wrote about it often. Peter knew it too, but had to go through a dreadful experience to be sure of it.

Not long after declaring that Jesus was the Messiah and watching the crowds celebrating Jesus' entry into Jerusalem, Peter assured Jesus that no matter what happened there, he would stand by his Messiah, even to the point of death.

Disastrously, Peter did not keep his promise. He denied even knowing Jesus when the pressure was on. In fact he denied knowing Jesus three times — hardly a careless, once-off slip.

Jesus was crucified and buried and three days later rose from the dead.

According to Mark's record in the New Testament, three women went to Jesus' tomb and discovered Jesus no longer there.
An angel told them he had risen and that they were to go and report this to the disciples, and to Peter.

I used to wonder why Peter was singled out.
Surely he was already included in "the disciples" the angel referred to, so why was special mention made of him?

I now think the angel was saying,
"Tell the disciples everything is OK. Jesus is risen.
And especially tell Peter, his failure to stand by Jesus has had no permanent effect. Tell him that it's all OK."

John recorded the occasion later on when Jesus personally caught up with Peter.
Three times Jesus asked Peter if he loved him and three times Jesus reinstated and recommissioned Peter to ministry in the future — once for each time Peter denied knowing him.

Jesus was telling him,
"Your failure hasn't changed anything between us.
You're still the person I've chosen to start my church.
Do you still love me?"

I reckon that's an interesting question.
Jesus asked Peter if *he* still loved him.

It was Peter who had let Jesus down; it might have been more natural to ask if Jesus still loved Peter.
But no, that was never in question.
Because Jesus is the Son of God, who *is* love, how could Jesus do anything less?

That ministry of Peter's commenced a few weeks later on the Day of Pentecost.
Peter's first sermon in the new Christian era, accompanied by a spectacular show of God's presence and power, saw God adding 3000 to those being saved at that time.

Regardless of Peter's previous performance, Jesus showed he still loved him, and was prepared to trust the beginnings of the Christian era to his leadership.

God loves us even when we fail him.
God is faithful to us even when we are not faithful to him.
The Bible shows us over and over that God is always in the reinstating, restoring and recommissioning business.
Even for those who have previously denied him.

Just another thought before we leave Peter.
If you know the incident where Peter denied knowing Jesus, you will remember that Jesus predicted this would happen and that a rooster would crow immediately afterwards.

Can you imagine how that denial might leap into Peter's mind every time he heard a rooster crow from that time onwards?
How terrible!
But how wonderful if at this time Peter also instantly remembered the love and forgiveness of Jesus too.

We do tend to forget, or take for granted, God's goodness to us.
We need reminders of those occasions otherwise we just take them for granted.

Some of us are healed from illnesses or injuries by God's miraculous intervention.
But after we have been well for a while, and life gets busy, we just forget how we became well and able to be busy with life again.

I know I do.
I have been healed many times, thanked God for his merciful touch, then just continued on my merry way.

But on one occasion, I was left with a small surface scar under which God's healing had taken place.
I am now so grateful for that scar, which I see every day in the shower, as it reminds me of the healing power of God and the way he used that power on me.

But even though we forget him, take him for granted, even deny him through that forgetfulness, he still loves us, forgives us and wants us to share in his kingdom or government work.
That's the sort of God I can worship and serve.

A Savage Monster

Many people genuinely doubt God's love for all humankind and cite examples from the Old Testament to demonstrate how savage God appears to have been in the past, and therefore is likely to be in the future.

Of all the examples used, the destruction of the whole world's population, less eight people, during the flood at the time of Noah is the most common.

How can God be a God of love and yet destroy everyone?

How can God, who *is* love, wipe the earth clean of almost all human beings in one fell swoop?

These are reasonable questions which many people, including Christians, find difficult to answer in a satisfactory way.

If we look at God's dealings with humankind through the lens of love, rather than through the lens of punishment and vengeance, we will see a different picture than many suppose.

Occasionally, we might hear a conversation between a person in authority and an alleged offender, or between a parent and a child, include words like, "I don't want you to say another word, you are in deep enough as it is."

In movies or television dramas we might hear a lawyer or attorney advising clients in a similar way so as not to risk providing more evidence against themselves or painting themselves in a worse light.

How can God be a God of love and yet destroy everyone?

Wise parents often advise their children to stay away from situations that would appeal to their weaknesses or make them susceptible to going astray.

People who are alcoholics are advised to not even have one alcoholic drink; people who are compulsive gamblers are advised to stay away from places that promote gambling; children who are more followers than leaders are advised to stay away from those who would have a detrimental influence on their lives.

It is wisdom and compassion that leads people to give this sort of advice to those they love.

Given that many of those who leave this planet at the end of their lives unreconciled to God will need to be judged and may spend time in "rehab" at the end of the ages, it was kind and merciful of God to prematurely remove from the planet those of Noah's generation who had made the world corrupt and full of violence before they could do even worse and be in need of an even more extreme and painful makeover.

And where did they go? And what happened to them there?
That's a wonderful story we will discuss a bit further on.
(If you've already caught a glimpse of the theme of this book, or have peeked ahead, you will know that the result was a very good one — much better than they, or any of us, deserve.)

But for the moment, those God "destroyed" were removed from the planet to prevent them from making things worse for themselves or leaving them where they could not resist the temptation to continue in their sinful ways.

This "clearing of the earth" was not the doings of a savage, vengeful God: it was the action of a loving and merciful God towards those he loves, not unlike that of a loving parent caring for his or her wayward children.

If we read or hear of any event in which God seems to be unreasonably harsh, let us pause for a moment and re-visit that event, looking at it through the lens of love.
If God *is* love, then what could he be doing here?
Viewing things this way makes a huge difference for me.

The Wise and Loving Parent

The big day arrived. Your son has just turned 6 and you arrange a birthday party for him in the back yard.

During the games and other activities your child makes a real pest of himself.
He is a poor loser when someone else wins a competition.
He has to have the first piece of cake going around, and the biggest piece at that.

He shows extreme displeasure with some of the presents he has been given.
He is a pain and is beginning to arouse anger and frustration in his guests.
The party is ready to explode.

Do you leave him continue this way, and risk ruining the party, and worse still, risk losing all his friends? Of course not.
You quietly take him from the yard and give him some "time out" in his room where others can't see him and where he can not make things any worse, for himself or for his friends.

Were you angry with what your son did? Most definitely.
Did you still love your son? Absolutely.
So, what will you do next?

After a certain length of time, you visit your son in his room, help him understand what has been happening and its present and possible future consequences, and help him change his attitude and future behaviour and to see the potential benefits that would come from these changes.

Those changes would also have the benefit of dissolving your anger and being reconciled to your son, moving on in harmony with him.

God watched on as his wayward creation behaved badly in the days of Noah.
He loved them, yet was angry with their behaviour.
He decided to remove them from the earth and give them some "time out" in Hades, where others couldn't see them.

Was God angry with what they did? Yes.
Did he make a judgement about their behaviour? Yes.
Did he destroy them — remove them from the earth? Yes.
Did he place them in Hades? Yes.
Did he love them? Yes.

Did he visit them later in their bedroom, in Hades? I think so.
Did he talk to them about how things could be better for them in the future? Probably.

If we can do these things well as sinful, earthly parents, how much better is God, as the most loving parent of all, at restoring his wayward and badly behaving offspring and teaching them to lead a life that is pleasing and reconciled to him?

So What About Death?

To some people God's statement that "the soul who sins will die", as recorded by the Old Testament prophet Ezekiel, and the Apostle Paul's statement that "the wages of sin is death", as recorded in the New Testament, are just further examples of God's nasty side.

What a spoil sport! What a harsh tyrant God is!

If we look at these through the lens of love rather than the lens of punishment and vengeance we again see God's good side, God's love.

After Adam and Eve sinned, God banished them from the garden so they could not eat from the tree of life in their sinful condition. God did not want them to live forever in such a fractured relationship with him.

Instead, they were to die, be removed from the garden, and eventually from the earth, until Jesus had come to earth and paid for their sin, and they could be restored to their original relationship with God.

In this way, strange as it might seem, death could be viewed as humankind's friend.
Those who lived in the "BC world" left the earth at the end of their lifetimes and waited in Hades (the unseen realm) for Jesus to deal with their sin at Calvary.

Those of us who live in the "AD world" are headed in one of two directions on our death.
Those who have been reconciled to God move to be with God.
Those who have not been reconciled to God go to face judgement and rehabilitation sometime in their future.

Either way God's love for his creation will prevail and all of humanity will be reconciled to him in the end, just like the naughty birthday boy was to his supervising parent.

Death is the doorway into the unseen and either directly or eventually to life, depending on whether people are reconciled to God during their time on this planet or not.
Thank God he allows us to die rather than live forever in our unreconciled condition.

An Overzealous Traffic Cop

Maybe you don't consider God to be a savage monster, but think he is more like an overzealous traffic cop, just waiting for us to break the rules before he pounces.

Suppose I am driving home enjoying the afternoon sun as I return from a fairly normal day at the office.
Occasionally I glance at the speedometer, check my mirrors and anticipate what may be ahead, but generally I am pretty relaxed and maybe a little carefree in my driving habits.

But today, on one of those glances in the rear vision mirror, I notice a traffic cop has appeared from nowhere and pulled into my lane — right behind me.
My demeanour and sense of peace immediately changes.
My heart beats a bit faster and questions race through my head.

How long has *he* been there?

God's Unconditional, Unfailing Love

Is my speed above what it should be?
Have I changed lanes without signalling?
Have I failed to give way to another car that had right-of-way?

My driving habits change.
I am now more careful.
I check my speed and mirrors more frequently.
My level of attention has upped significantly.
My concentration is on high alert.

I am now "back at work" rather than taking a leisurely, relaxing drive home.

Why have all these changes happened?
Simple — I'm afraid.
I am driven by the fear of doing something wrong and the consequences that will bring.

Even though I know the cop is there to keep me, and others, safe on the road, am I endeared to him? Do I love him? Not likely.
The best I can say is that I respect his position and authority.
But more truthfully, I fear him and fear what he can do to me.

And, O, how relieved I am when I see him disappear from my field of view, having turned off at the intersection I just crossed.
Heart rate back to normal, sitting more relaxed behind the wheel, level of concentration back to leisure level ... phew!

That's how many people relate to God.
It was the norm in Old Testament times, and too often the norm today, even among Christians.

We fear God and what he can do to us because of the mistakes we have made, continue to make, and will probably make in the future — and because we don't know him very well.

In one regional city where I lived, I got to know a traffic cop really well through business and church connections.
I would see him on the roads quite often and sometimes he would be in my lane travelling right behind me.

My driving skills made the usual improvements when he was around so that I wouldn't do anything wrong.

But it wasn't because I feared him or feared what he could do to me.
I just didn't want to embarrass him or give him the unpleasant task of having to make any hard decisions about me.

I respected his position and authority as much as any other cop in town, but I cared about him and didn't want to make his life or job more difficult because of his relationship with me.

It was interesting to note that although my driving improved when he was around, my heart rate didn't increase nor did my sense of peace evaporate.
I was in the same relaxed state as when the road was free of traffic cops — just my attention to my driving improved.

It was easy to see that I performed better on the road when he was around.
But it was because I loved him and cared for him, not because I feared him.
Same result on the road — but for entirely different reasons.
My love for him removed the need for me to fear him.
Fear just wasn't relevant.
Driving improvement occurred without it.

Fearing God has us behaving better, and that was the point of the

law for those who lived under it in Old Testament times.
It was better for each individual and for society as a whole.

But Jesus came to move us beyond that law and to show us that God is love and desires a relationship of love with each of us.
If we love him we will want to live the way he desires us to.
And there will be no room or need for fear in that relationship.
In fact the Bible says that perfect love drives out fear.

How much better is it to realise that God really does love us and invites us into a relationship of love with him — better than living in fear that God might pounce on us when we don't meet the full requirements of the law.

Some Serious Questions

Jesus told us to love our enemies and do good to them.
In this way, he said, we would be showing that we were children of God, who is kind to the ungrateful and wicked.
Jesus then instructed us to be merciful, just as God is merciful.

Why then do so many Christians, and others, expect that God will torment his enemies forever in a place they call hell, if Jesus said God is the perfect model of kindness and mercy?

How come many Christians say that God loves everyone unconditionally, then immediately begin to list the conditions under which that love can be received?
"You must love God back" and "You must do this or that before you die and leave this planet" are the two most common conditions listed.

Where do people get the idea that God's unconditional love for us is dependent on where we are or what we do?
How absurd to think we can control God, or his attitude, in any way at all!

Most Christians believe that "Jesus Christ is the same yesterday, today and forever", but are not prepared to extend that "sameness" to his love for sinners.

If Jesus loved, welcomed and accepted sinners while he was on this planet, why won't he continue to do that, regardless of where they are or where he is?

Where do people get the idea that someone's location changes God's love for them or changes his desire to save them?

These questions continue to puzzle and frustrate me.
While I'm working on my questions, how about you having a go at these.

Are you a parent? If so ...

> Do you love your kids?
> Do you ever discipline them? Why?
> What is the purpose of your discipline?
> How severe is your discipline?
> Does it ever stop? When?
> Does it achieve its purpose?

(Even if you're not a parent, you'll probably be able to offer good answers as an observer to the parenting you've seen in families you know.
So don't skip over the challenge. Go back and have a go too.)

Now we are all ready to have a go at the following questions together.

> Does God love his offspring (the people who populate his earth)?
> Does he ever discipline them? Why?
> What is the purpose of his discipline?
> How severe is his discipline?

Does it ever stop? When?
Does it achieve its purpose?

Definition of Love

Do you realise we are well into a chapter on love and still haven't even talked about what love is. So ... just pause reading, and ask yourself ... what is this thing we call love?

Seriously, did you pause and do that?
So what did you decide? What is your definition of love?

I have a very simple definition of love — simple to explain, that is, but much harder to live by.
For me, to love someone is to genuinely desire the best for them — and as the opportunity arises, to do that best for them.
That works for me, and is another way of saying what the Bible says.

> *If you love others, you will never do them wrong;*
> *[Romans 13 : 10 GNT]*

Which is fair enough.
Surely if love can only love, it can't do anything that is unloving. It's not that it chooses not to or feels it shouldn't — it just can't!

But the Bible has something even more detailed.

> *Love is patient, love is kind.*
> *It does not envy, it does not boast, it is not proud. It does not dishonour others, it is not self-seeking, it is not easily angered, it keeps no record of wrongs.*
> *Love does not delight in evil but rejoices with the truth.*
> *It always protects, always trusts, always hopes, always perseveres.*
> *Love never fails.*
> *[1 Corinthians 13 : 4 — 8 NIV]*

Given that the Bible says that God *is* love, we can make that substitution in these verses to produce a most informative description of God.

> *God is patient, God is kind.*
> *God does not envy, God does not boast,*
> *God is not proud.*
> *God does not dishonour others, God is not self-seeking, God is not easily angered, God keeps no record of wrongs.*
> *God does not delight in evil but rejoices with the truth.*
> *God always protects, always trusts, always hopes, always perseveres.*
> *God never fails.*

This substitution produces a version of the Corinthian description of love that gives us a picture of God and his love.
And the connection that God, who *is* love, loves in this way leads me to the conclusion that understanding love is the key to understanding God.

It's a bit like the sun in our solar system. The sun not only radiates light, it *is* light. It is the very source of light. There would be no light if there were no sun.

Sometimes the sun is hidden from us by clouds or curtains on our windows, and can even be misrepresented by coloured or obscure glass, but it always exists in its correct form, with its correct character and performing its correct role.

Unfortunately, God is too often obscured from us or misrepresented to us as well.
In our more sober moments we know that God *is* love, but we often allow people or circumstances to misrepresent him, and even obscure him.

Although we have heard it said many, many times that God *is* love, how many of us truly believe ...

> that God is patient and kind,
> that God is not easily angered,
> that God keeps no record of wrongs,
> that God always perseveres,
> that God's love never fails?

... to love someone is to genuinely desire the best for them ...

Good mothers demonstrate these standards of love all the time.
Why should we assume God demonstrates a lesser quality of love than the mothers he created?
If God *is* love, the source of love, he cannot help himself when it comes to loving. He is always in the loving business.

The Bible really nails it when it says:

> *This is how we know what love is: Jesus Christ gave his life for us.*
> [1 John 3 : 16 GNT]

It's because we don't understand love that we often think that God deserts us or that he acts unlovingly toward us.
We admit that even with our best attempts there are some people we just do not love.

There are also times when we don't truly love the people we usually love — at least not as generously as we ought.
And we judge God's performance and even his desire by our own.
But that is surely to misrepresent it, and even obscure it, either from ourselves or from others.

Many of our stresses and fears would disappear if we truly knew God loves us, and that this love is pure, unblemished, unchanging and unending.

To see God and to know him is made much easier if we just remove, or look beyond, the obstacles that obscure him or misrepresent him.

The Law of Gravity

I enjoy reading science.
Although my science degree (from more than 50 years ago) is in Physics, I like to keep in touch with where humankind is up to in appreciating and understanding God's wonderful creation in other areas as well — like chemistry, biology, geology and astronomy.
So please indulge me and let me digress a little to talk some science.

Newton's Universal Law of Gravitation states that any two objects exert a gravitational force of attraction on each other.
The direction of that force is from the centre of one object to the centre of the other.
The size of the force is determined by the size of the objects and their distance apart.

For any two particular objects the force on one is the same as the force on the other, but the effect of that force will be more visible on the smaller object.

Let me illustrate by considering these two objects — the earth and me. We attract each other with a force of about 800 "force units" (in the metric measurement system). If I step off the top of a building, removing the "obstacle" between the earth and me, this force causes us to come together quite rapidly.
But which one of us does the moving?
The force of 800 force units is not enough to get the earth moving towards me, but it sure moves me towards the earth.

So, small objects will move towards, and may eventually collide with, large objects because the force of attraction between them gets the smaller one moving more easily.

So why this digression? I knew you'd be wondering by now.
I see the law of love working in the same way as the law of gravitation.
They are both universal laws put in place by God — one in the physical realm and one in the spiritual.

In the universal law of love, God is the big object and humankind is the small one.
There is a love force of attraction between God and us whose direction is from the centre or heart of God to our centres or hearts.
That force is always acting so that when obstacles between us and God are reduced or removed, we will start moving towards God — and will eventually meet him, be united with him.

Jesus referred to this when he said that he would draw all people to himself.
It might take a while, it might need several obstacles to be removed, maybe reduced piece by piece, but eventually all people will meet him and be united with him.

Although it can be dangerous to take parables or illustrations too far, let me continue this thought a bit further.
You will remember that I said the size of the gravitational force of attraction between objects is influenced by the distance between them.

> *God's influence on humankind is never zero, no matter how far from God any person might be.*

Without getting immersed in the mathematics involved, it should be obvious that the greater the distance between them, the less will be the size of the force — the further they are apart, the less influence they will have on each other.

When an astronaut is in outer space, the distance between him and the earth is so great that a feeling of weightlessness is experienced.

The force between them, the weight force experienced, is thought to be zero. Mathematically, this is not correct as the force can never reduce to nothing at all.
But the force is so small that the astronaut is not aware of it.

Equally, with the law of love.
God's influence on humankind is never zero, no matter how far from God any person might be.
Reason requires this to be so, and the Bible assures us of this truth.

If God is God, the Creator of all there is, he must be touchable from any and every part of his universe.
A creator just has to have his creation within his sphere of influence.

The Bible declares it this way.

> Where could I go to escape from you?
> Where could I get away from your presence?
> If I went up to heaven, you would be there;
> if I lay down in the world of the dead, you would be there.
> If I flew away beyond the east or lived in the farthest place in the west, you would be there to lead me, you would be there to help me.
> I could ask the darkness to hide me or the light around me to turn into night, but even darkness is not dark for you, and the night is as bright as the day. Darkness and light are the same to you.
> [Psalm 139 : 7 — 12 GNT]

Isn't it good to know God stays in touch with us — even though we might not be aware of it?

Yes, God really does love us.

He came to earth in an earth-suit and was known by the name "Jesus" to show us that the core of his nature and character is love and that he was prepared to pay the ultimate price a person on earth could pay to prove that.

He wants the best for us and has already done the best for us as well — for all of us.

Too much of traditional Christian teaching presents a God who *has* love, or loves to a certain degree, or loves those who love him in return, but is rarely presented as someone who *is* love — who *is* the love that never fails.

With that understanding under our belts, let's continue building the "specs" that will guide our thinking and discussions about his plans.

Chapter Two will put in the second lens, God is Lord or Sovereign.
Let's get right on to it.

CHAPTER 2

God's Supreme Sovereignty

IN August 2011, bloody riots erupted across the United Kingdom. Wanton destruction and arson, unprovoked violence, civil disobedience and rebellion, looting on a grand scale, and a growing death toll made daily news around the world.

Riots somewhere in the world are nothing new, I hear you say.
Yes, but in the UK? It took me by surprise.
I thought the only rioting that happened in the UK was at football matches, and even this had been curtailed in recent years due to wide-scale government crackdowns.
The video footage we saw being updated by the hour during that month shocked most of us.

In some parts of the world wars, riots and civil unrest are a way of life. If you doubt such a broad generalisation, have a look at *http://en.wikipedia.org/wiki/List_of_wars* and *http://en.wikipedia.org/wiki/List_of_riots*.

Then add to those lists ...
the enormous work loads of our law enforcement officers and courts, the staggering number of new laws our parliaments enact each year in their efforts to curb the destructive immoral and criminal forces in our societies, the number of domestic and workplace disputes and acts of violence we read about in our local newspapers or hear about on our TV networks, ...
and we soon get an idea of the mess our world is in.

On a more personal level, we all know that life can be difficult, downright painful — unhappy marriages, miscarried pregnancies, grief over wayward children, losing a job, terminal illnesses, unfulfilled careers, racial discrimination, social rejection — the list is never ending.

Aware of these painful realities, it is easy for questions like

> "Does God exist? Doesn't he care?"
> "Is God really in control? Of everything?"

to tease, or even torment us.

And if the answer to these questions is "Yes", other questions immediately surface.

> "How do we explain the sin and evil in the world?"
> "Why doesn't God intervene?"
> "Why is life so tough and unfair?"

These are top questions and the answers to them have been debated for centuries.
Some people blame God for the state the world is in; some blame humankind in general; some blame Adam and Eve; some blame nature; most of us have no answers at all.

Nevertheless, it intrigues me that people who study the Bible looking for answers to these important questions often end up with completely different points of view.

Earlier we mentioned that one of Christianity's most commonly held beliefs is the endless punishment or torture in a place usually called "hell" for all who fail to be reconciled to God through a personal relationship with Jesus Christ before they leave this planet.

If that scenario is true, then these questions must also be faced.

> "How can endless torture bring credit to God?"
> "How can that be for every person's well-being?"
> "Where does a God of unfailing love fit with that final outcome?"
> "What does this say about the care of a loving Father?"
> "What does it say about the value of Jesus' sacrifice for the world's sin?"

As you can see this is going to be an interesting chapter. Regardless of the different points of view that people get from the Bible, it is still the place to go for answers to such big questions.

Even if you're already familiar with the Bible, I reckon we'll have some surprises for you before we get to the end of this chapter.

God's Sovereignty

Until my retirement, I have been in leadership positions all my life, even as a teenager. I can't recall ever seeking those positions or promoting myself for them. Quite the opposite in fact.

I still remember being nominated for the position of class captain when I was just 12 years of age, but didn't vote for myself in the ensuing election as I thought to do so would have been an improper thing to do. (I lost the election by one vote — mine.)

Those leadership positions have covered a wide range of settings and jurisdictions.
From local to city-wide to state-wide; from governance to management to operational; from small business to corporate to political to religious.
So I guess I know a little about leadership, about being at the top of the tree.
Yet, I know nothing about sovereignty, about owning the forest.

So let's explore what the sovereignty of God, what owning the forest, is all about.
Here's a sample of the revelations God has given some of the greats of the Bible era.
The Psalms in several places include statements like this one ...

> The LORD does whatever pleases him in the heavens
> and on the earth, in the seas and all their depths.
> [Psalm 135 : 6 NIV]

From Solomon — considered to be the wisest man to have ever lived, said ...

> The Lord controls the mind of a king as easily as he directs the course of a stream.
> [Proverbs 21 : 1 NIV]

Isaiah — the famous Israelite prophet — described God this way ...

> ... the Creator of the heavens, who stretches them out, who spreads out the earth with all that springs from it,
> who gives breath to its people, and life to those who walk on it:

and then quotes God in this way ...

> "I am the LORD; that is my name!
> I will not yield my glory to another
> or my praise to idols."

> *"I am the Lord, and there is no other;*
> *apart from me there is no God ..."*
>
> *"... I am God, and there is no other;*
> *I am God, and there is none like me.*
> *I make known the end from the beginning,*
> *From ancient times, what is still to come.*
>
> *I say, 'My purpose will stand,*
> *and I will do all that I please.'*
> *From the east I summon a bird of prey;*
> *From a far-off land, a man to fulfil my purpose.*
>
> *What I have said, that I will bring about;*
> *what I have planned, that I will do."*
> [Isaiah 42 : 5, 8 and 45 : 5 and 46 : 9 — 11 NIV]

Sounds pretty much like God does as he chooses.
If God is the Creator-Owner of the universe and in full control of it, why shouldn't he?
And we'll see how this is worked out in the lives of the people I call "the J men" a bit later.

Some of these quotations remind me of a movie I saw a few years back. It was called *Bella* and was based on a true love story about how events that happened one day in New York City changed the lives of three people forever.

As the opening titles were being shown, Jose, the hero of the story, was heard to say in a quiet voice-over,

> *"My grandmother used to say,*
> *'If you want to make God laugh, tell him your plans.'"*

I have never forgotten that line.
I think Solomon would also agree.

He said,

> "People may plan all kinds of things,
> but the Lord's will is going to be done."
> [Proverbs 19 : 21 GNT]

Have you ever thought about the consequences of God *not* being sovereign, of God *not* being in control?
It raises the prospect that any of his plans can be undone at any time.
He might be over-ruled by someone or something else.
Something might turn up that he wasn't expecting, that catches him off-guard.
His plan to save the world through Jesus might be unravelled or circumvented in the future.
The possibilities are endless — and way too scary to think about.

He just *has* to be sovereign or he is not God.
Just as God *is* love, he *is* sovereign or Lord.

I wonder how many of us have a secret, underlying hope that God might just be sovereign.
Although we might not admit it, the increase in church attendance in times of national crisis and tragedy might suggest that this is so.

It is well documented that after the 9/11 terrorist attacks in the United States, church attendance increased dramatically.
Church attendance in Britain and the USA also surged during the Second World War.

Does this say something about a hidden or unexpressed belief that many people have in the sovereignty of God which pops up its head at desperate times like these?
Or is it just a hope of last resort?

Satan and Evil

Here's a good question.
If God is the Creator-Owner of all and is in control of all he created, then what about Satan and evil? (By "evil" I am meaning the opposite of peace and well-being, opposites like calamity, disaster, trouble, unrest, discord and misfortune.)

That question raises some confronting possibilities, doesn't it?
Since God created all things, the heavens and the earth and everything in them, could this also mean he created evil and the Devil, or Satan?

Have you ever thought about the consequences of God not being sovereign, of God not being in control?

The Bible says that

> *Christ is the visible likeness of the invisible God. He is the first-born Son, superior to all created things.*
> *For through him God created everything in heaven and on earth, the seen and the unseen things, including spiritual powers, lords, rulers, and authorities.*
> *God created the whole universe through him and for him.*
> *[Colossians 1 : 15 — 16 GNT]*

And since all things were not only created by him, but *for* him, then isn't it possible that evil and Satan were created *for* God to use, to achieve some planned purpose?
And since God is love, surely that purpose would have to be a good one?

Remembering that God is the playwright of the Grand Stage Production who chose the role and character of each of its actors, why wouldn't some of those actors be cast in villainous roles to flesh out the story-line?

And why wouldn't evil, wrong-doing, and natural disasters be possible events along the way? Even insurance companies refer to natural disasters as "acts of God".

We won't stray too far into God's purpose right now (that's the focus of Chapter Three), but let's explore this intriguing possibility before *rigour mortis* sets in and you cannot read any further.

Christian thought has often promoted the idea that Satan was created a beautiful, highly placed angel in heaven who somehow became proud and rebellious and led an army of angels in revolt against God.
God won the battle however, and booted Satan out of heaven and down to the earth.
In his demoted state, Satan introduced evil into our world, and continues to promote it and sponsor his revolution among humankind to the present day.

This standard "status quo" story about evil and Satan is a comforting view as it avoids accusing God of creating anything other than good. However, the Bible seems to confirm the unthinkable proposition that God did indeed create all things in heaven and on earth, including evil.

> *... I am the Lord, and there is no other.*
> *I form the light and create darkness,*
> *I bring prosperity and create disaster;*
> *I, the Lord, do all these things.*
> *[Isaiah 45 : 6 — 7 NIV]*
>
> *Who can speak and have it happen if the Lord has not decreed it? Is it not from the mouth of the Most High that both calamities and good things come?*
> *[Lamentations 3 : 37 — 38 NIV]*

> *Consider what God has done:*
> *Who can straighten what he has made crooked?*
> *When times are good be happy;*
> *but when times are bad, consider this:*
> *God has made the one as well as the other...*
> *[Ecclesiastes 7 : 13 — 14 NIV]*

I don't have any problem believing a "good" God creates evil if his purpose in doing so is good.
Indeed, as we have just seen, if we read the Bible carefully, it tells us that God is the author of evil — disaster, calamities, bad times.

Now what about Satan? Did God create him too?
If he didn't, then who did? Satan couldn't have created himself! And the Bible says that God created *all* things through Jesus Christ.

But what sort of being did God create him?
As a perfect, beautiful angel that went astray or as a villain right from the start?

The Bible calls Satan

> *"... the ruler of the kingdom of the air, the spirit who is now at work in those who are disobedient."*
> *[Ephesians 2 : 2 NIV]*

Jesus says about Satan,

> *"He was a murderer from the beginning,*
> *not holding to the truth, for there is no truth in him.*
> *When he lies, he speaks his native language,*
> *for he is a liar and the father of lies."*
> *[John 8 : 44 NIV]*

So the Bible says he is a spirit being who has been a villain right from the beginning.
And if that is so, it seems that God must have created him that way!

Since anyone who creates anything always has a purpose for their creation, it doesn't make sense to suggest that God would have no purpose in creating evil and Satan.
So why did God do it?

I think there are two main reasons.
Firstly, God uses Satan and evil to demonstrate his own character.
Have you ever wondered what we would know about light, if each 24 hour day was always light, and was never anything else?
Light would be assumed, not thought about; it would be taken as "just the way things are".
It would be taken for granted until an alternative was presented, until we were deprived of it for some time.
Once we have experienced darkness, an alternative or opposite to light, we gain an immediate understanding and appreciation of light.

Oxygen fits into this category too.
No-one consciously thinks about their need of oxygen or goes out of their way to make sure they are getting this vital element.
But if we are put in a situation where the oxygen supply is depleted or cut off entirely, we suddenly discover how valuable and desirable it is.

Good health illustrates this principle as well.
We go merrily along doing everything we want to do, however we want to do it, until one day we find ourselves ill — deprived of the good health we had previously taken for granted.
Life suddenly changes and we realise what we have just lost.
Not thinking about good health changes to appreciating and desiring it.
Our illness shows us very clearly what good health was.

And it's not difficult to think of many other examples.
I live in a beautiful, stable, wealthy democracy called Australia.
We grumble about little things like the weather, petty government decisions, umpiring decisions in sporting events, and the price of petrol — and think we are hardly done by.

Many Australians travel overseas and often visit countries with barren landscapes and harsh climates where extreme poverty, social crime and government instability and corruption are the norm. When these travellers arrive home their first comment is usually something like, "I'll never grumble about Australia again. You don't realise how well off we are until you see how others have to live."

Adam and Eve had a similar experience to the travelling Aussies. They were enjoying God's perfect provision for them and intimate relationship with him, but obviously did not realise just how good things were ... until they had to do without them.

Without the contrast, Adam and Eve took God for granted, didn't value who he was or the magnificent paradise in which they lived, and wanted to buck the system to "improve" their lot.

Contrasts provided by the "bad" help us fully understand and appreciate the value in the "good".
God uses contrasts all the time — uses the bad to help us see his good.

> *To understand and appreciate God's love, goodness ... God knows we need to experience their absence or opposite.*

How would we know the true value of love without being exposed to hate, or some other reduced dose of love?
Would we ever understand good without being exposed to evil, the absence of good?
What would we know about health, if it were not for sickness?
And about wealth, if it were not for the existence of poverty?

To understand and appreciate God's love, goodness, mercy, grace and forgiveness God knows we need to experience their absence or opposite.

Secondly, God uses Satan and evil to prepare his "early believers" for leadership in the coming ages.
That can sound a bit strange to some of us.
However, a few pages on we will see examples of this in the lives of two famous Bible characters, Job and Joseph.

God used Satan to harass Job and perfect and strengthen his faith, while God used the evil intentions of Joseph's brothers to put Joseph in a position to save the fledgling Israeli nation from starvation and possible extinction.

But before we get there, let's see some incidents recorded in the New Testament in which evil and Satan are used for a similar purpose.

Jesus himself was tempted (tested) in the Judean desert or wilderness by Satan.
The Bible records report ...

> *Then Jesus was led by the Spirit into the wilderness to be tempted by the devil.*
> *[Matthew 4 : 1 NIV]*

Did you notice that this circumstance didn't just happen?
How did Jesus get into the desert?
Wow! God led him there so he could use Satan to test him.

And, of course, as he continued his life on this planet he experienced some awful sufferings along the way.
The Bible describes their purpose this way ...

> *But even though he was God's Son, he learned obedience through his sufferings.*
> *When he was made perfect, he became the source of salvation through the ages for all who obey him,*
> *[Hebrews 5 : 8 — 9 BV]*

How about that!

It is a great application of God using the bad to show the true value of the good.
And to show humankind that Jesus was perfectly obedient, God decided to demonstrate that Jesus could remain obedient even under the most horrendous persecution and suffering.
Which, of course, he did to pay the price for our sin.

Jesus told the church at Smyrna that some of them would experience similar treatment to his, and for similar reasons.

> *Do not be afraid of what you are about to suffer.*
> *I tell you, the devil will put some of you in prison to*
> *test you, and you will suffer persecution for ten days.*
> *Be faithful, even to the point of death,*
> *and I will give you life as your victor's crown.*
> *[Revelation 2 : 10 NIV]*

Paul "gave" people over to Satan to help them clean up their act and become better people.

Look at this example ... Paul is advising Timothy to be

> *holding on to faith and a good conscience,*
> *which some have rejected and so have suffered*
> *shipwreck with regard to the faith.*
>
> *Among them are Hymenaeus and Alexander,*
> *whom I have handed over to Satan to be taught not*
> *to blaspheme.*
> *[1 Timothy 1 : 19 – 20 NIV]*

and tells the Corinthians to do the same with the man in their church who had been sexually immoral.

> *hand this man over to Satan for the destruction of*
> *the flesh, so that his spirit may be saved on the day*
> *of the Lord.*
> *[1 Corinthians 5 : 5 NIV]*

As an interesting aside, God's law plays a similar role.
I am not saying that God's law is evil, but that God uses it in a similar way to how he uses evil.

The law shows us the standards that God expects of us together with the price to be paid for not meeting those standards.
And it is certain that we will not meet them — we are really not up to the challenge.
God's grace, without these standards and penalties staring us in the face, would be grossly undervalued, if appreciated at all.

No-one can be declared trustworthy until they have defeated the temptation to be untrustworthy.
No-one can be assumed strong until they have been tested for weakness.

In the same way, no-one can be declared victorious or an overcomer until they have faced an enemy — and won!

God's purpose is to give his "early believers" obstacles to overcome, whether evil or good like the law.
We learn how to live powerfully as we access the overcoming power of the Holy Spirit.

Willy Wonka

Have you seen the movie *Willy Wonka and the Chocolate Factory?* Yes? How long ago?
Do you remember the closing scenes in the 1971 version (with Gene Wilder playing Wonka)?

Grandpa Joe and Charlie Bucket are meeting with Willy Wonka in Willy's office (where everything is cut in half). During the previous tour of the factory, each of the children had been given an everlasting gobstopper as a gift from Wonka on condition that they not give it away.

Grandpa, in his anger, threatens to give Charlie's gobstopper to Slugworth, the character who had been so desperate and cunning in trying to get hold of one.
Instead, Charlie places his gobstopper on Willy's desk, demonstrating his faithfulness in completing the task Willy had originally given him.

Willy excitedly bursts out with …
"So shines a good deed in a weary world.
Charlie … my boy … You won! You did it! You did it! I knew you would; I just knew you would.
Oh, Charlie, forgive me for putting you through this.
Please, forgive me.
Come in, Mr Wilkinson. Charlie, meet Mr Wilkinson."

As Mr Wilkinson enters, Charlie immediately recognises him and exclaims, "Slugworth!".
"No, no, that's not Slugworth. He works for me," replies Willy.
"For you?"
"I had to test you, Charlie. And you passed the test. You won!" announces Willy.

"Won what?" asks Grandpa Joe.
"The jackpot, my dear sir, the grand and glorious jackpot."
"The chocolate?" asks Charlie.
"The chocolate, yes, the chocolate, but that's just the beginning."

Charlie's disobedience in drinking the fizzy lifting drink was not counted against him.
Because he had clung to his everlasting gobstopper and had not betrayed Wonka, he was given chocolate for life *and* he inherited the chocolate factory as well.

Willy had used one of his employees (Mr Wilkinson portrayed as Slugworth up until now) to help him sort out who would be worthy to win this prize and to run the factory the way he wanted.

In God's realm, Satan is no more than one of God's employees.
God uses him to determine how we react to the thoughts and temptations that are whispered into our ears.

Those who pass the test, and hold on to their everlasting gobstopper, not only get the chocolate (life during the ages) but inherit the factory (the kingdom or government) as well.
The Bible calls these the "overcomers".

Clearly, both God and his employees (including Satan) play for the same team, with God as the captain, although not all employees seem to realise whose team they are really on.
God is truly sovereign over all.

What About Freewill?

That's another good question.
If God is the Creator-Owner of all and is in control of all he created, then where does this thing called "freewill" fit into the picture?
I know humankind's freewill is proudly proclaimed in the world, indeed highly valued and promoted in many Christian churches.

But let me say something else that might shock you.
Freewill is a myth.
Not the "will" part, but the "free" part.
As Dan Sheridan, of *Sheridan Voice (http://sheridanvoice.com)*, says, "There is only room for one person to have freewill in this universe — and it's not us."

God, in his sovereignty, has given us the authority and ability to make choices in many areas of our lives, but those choices are never made freely.
They are never free from one sort of influence or another.

Our heritage, our culture, education, personality, health, family values, beliefs and world view, and our current circumstances are constantly influencing the decisions we make.

How can we have freewill when all these influences are at play? And we haven't included the likely influences of Satan and evil, or even God, in the list!

Whether we acknowledge him or not, God is the supreme, overarching influence in the universe, as we have seen in the discussion above.
It is his universe, and he calls the shots in the end.
And let's think about this.

> *Free will is a myth.*
> *Not the "will" part but the "free" part.*

If all people are to be judged fairly
    and
if people's "eventual destinies" are at stake
    and
if such a thing as freewill really exists,
then it would be necessary for all people to be given a level playing field from birth.

But that is obviously not the case — all people do not have the same opportunities and choices.
Freewill is not a fair go if final results depend entirely on the choices we are able to make.

So for just these two reasons alone — external influences and the need to be fair to all — maybe we should abandon, or at least modify, our concept of human freewill.

One of the most famous Biblical characters was the Apostle Paul, originally known as Saul of Tarsus.
You will find me quoting from his writings, as recorded in the Bible, quite often.

He was given wonderful insights into God's purpose and plans that few others before him were privileged to know.
And his life story completely demolishes this mythical concept of freewill.

You can read about a major crossroads event in Paul's life in the Bible, in Acts Chapter 9.
Don't have a Bible? That's OK.
Hop onto the net, point to *Bible Gateway (www.biblegateway.com)* and type "Acts 9" in the Search Box.
The text of Acts Chapter 9 will be displayed in the centre of the page that appears below the box.

Paul thought he was serving God by hunting and imprisoning the followers of Jesus.
He was on his way to Damascus on another of these missions when God grabbed his attention in a spectacular way.
When a dazzling light shone, he was blinded, thrown to the ground and heard a voice speak from heaven.

How much freewill do you think Paul had at his disposal right then?
How much would we have had?
He could certainly make choices, but they were severely limited by the circumstances over which he had no control.

Nevertheless, he immediately chose to follow the directions he was given by Jesus and became his most loyal follower and enthusiastic ambassador.

Many of us have seen sci-fi movies where robots and other manufactured "smart" creatures at some point in their existence turn on their creators.
Their wills are unrestrained and eventually directed towards making decisions that cause mayhem and destruction that is totally opposed to their maker's will and purpose.

We watch and think to ourselves, "Why don't the scientists who created these beasts just pull out their plugs?"
We inherently believe the creator should have the final say, should be in control.

Freewill then is a mythical concept, created by humankind to express its deep longing to rebel against any form of authority or the need to be accountable to anyone but itself.

I like this thought from Aaron Locker, a regular contributor at *Bible Student's Notebook (http://biblestudentsnotebook.com)*.

> *A sovereign God is never subject to anything, especially not something that he has made out of the dust of the ground.*

So what should we call this thing that most others call "freewill"? God in his sovereignty has delegated to us the authority to rule — to make decisions and be responsible — in a defined arena, which I liken to a fenced paddock.

We have "limited freewill" — freewill within limits — and God encourages us to exercise that freewill within the limits or boundaries he has set.
Isn't that a beautiful oxymoron — "limited freewill"?
And very confronting to most of humankind, those creatures of the dust of the ground who think God is subject to their wills and the decisions they make.

As a loving father, God puts limits on our decision-making, as any responsible parent does.
Responsible parenting includes exposing children to the dangers of life in a controlled way under close supervision.
God doesn't allow us to destroy ourselves, but allows us to experience the bad of life — sin and pain and loneliness and malfunctioning bodies — under his close supervision.

In many cases, it sometimes takes a long, long time for children, ours and his, to appreciate the love and goodness of parents.
But good parent that God is, and continues to be, he does not give us "unlimited" freewill.

Horses Need Paddocks with Good Fences

One of my keen interests in the not-for-profit, corporate world was the connection between governance and management.
Because I have held both governance and management positions at various times in different organisations, I was in a fairly unique position to see the strengths and weaknesses of the operational models most often used.

The model I advocated focussed on keeping the governance and management responsibilities of the organisation clearly separate.
To avoid the dual problems of micro-management by the governance body and the lack of opportunity and scope for dynamic initiative-taking and decision-making by management, I promoted the horse and paddock model used by the Canadian not-for-profit governance expert John Carver.

Rather than several people having a rope around the horse's neck, one pulling this way and one pulling that, the horse is free to do anything it chooses as long as it stays inside the paddock.
Its freewill is limited by the fence.

The horse is restricted in a global way by what it could *not* do, rather than being forced to respond to the individual requirements of those who held a rope.

The application to the organisation was clear and freeing for both governance and management.
Rather than governance being overly prescriptive about how management should fulfil its function, the governance group was

required to build a fence by clearly prescribing the goals and outcomes to be achieved and proscribing the actions and practices to be avoided.

Governance was free to build the fence in any way it chose (governance was sovereign) but management was then free to function inside the fence in any way it chose (management had delegated authority and the freedom to use it responsibly).

As well as using this model in a governance-management environment, I also used it in a senior management-middle management setting.
In my senior management roles, I would prescribe the goals and desired outcomes, and proscribe the unacceptable actions and practices, for the managers under me, and they were then free to achieve those outcomes and avoid those restrictions in whatever ways they chose.

I set the game plan and enjoyed seeing the results roll in.
In between those two ends, the staff enjoyed doing their thing in their way and taking responsibility for their successes — and making me happy too.

Although I didn't appreciate it at the time, I later saw that this model was very close to a Biblical one.
In fact, it is similar to the model God uses in his dealings with us. And solves the sovereignty-freewill dilemma that so divides the Christian landscape.

Let's draw the paddock and fences again and use it to illustrate the relationship between God's will and ours.
I appreciate this illustration oversimplifies the situation somewhat, but I hope it helps to further our understanding.

God is the governing body, the sovereign authority, who designs and builds the fence in any way he chooses.
All decisions made outside the fence are made by God and describe the outcomes to be achieved and the activities to be avoided.

Humankind is the management team, confined to the paddock inside the fence, with authority delegated to it by God to make the decisions there.
These decisions and choices determine how successfully we achieve the outcomes and avoid the prohibited activities.

When we see it like this, it is clear that humankind does not have freewill at all.
We have the freedom to exercise our wills inside the fenced area — to use our "limited freewill".

The Magic Combo

So there is a magic combination that God has put in place which is a fine balance between two different authorities — God's sovereign authority and our delegated authority.

God has sovereign authority in his universe and is accountable to himself for exercising that authority responsibly.
He cannot let himself down, so has to achieve all his purposes and plans to be fully accountable.

On the other hand, we have delegated authority, a limited authority delegated to us by God and we are accountable to him for how we exercise it.

The ways these two authorities play themselves out and interact are seen in numerous situations in life and in the Bible, and are particularly illustrated by those I call "the J Men".

The J Men

I appreciate that many readers may not be familiar with the stories of the J men from the Bible.
For the longer stories, the ones about Job and Joseph, I'll give a short description to set the scene.
For Jonah, I'll invite you to read his very brief story for yourself before we discuss it.

Job's Story

The story of Job is recorded in the Bible in the book simply called "Job".
Job was a righteous man who lost everything — his wealth, his family and his health — and wrestled with the big "why?" question that so many of us face at times.

Unknown to Job, the disasters that confronted him had been designed by Satan after an agreement was struck between God and Satan in heaven.

> *We have delegated authority, a limited authority delegated to us by God.*

Job had three friends who came to comfort him, but they ended up just arguing over the reasons for Job's suffering.

In the end, Job and God shared some home truths, and after Job got his frustration off his chest and God had straightened him out, Job declared

> *I know that you can do all things, no purpose of yours can be thwarted.*
> [Job 42 : 2 NIV]

After Job acknowledged the sovereignty of God in his life, he received back more than he had lost.
Job was a transformed man after the experience, and learned that

God could use suffering to perfect even a so-called "righteous" person.

God's ultimate plan is to bring his creation to perfection, to Christ-likeness, and Job's story demonstrates how flexible God can be in pursuing his objective.

Satan wanted to torment Job and cause him to lose his trust in God.
God used Satan's mischievous scheme to make Job even stronger in his faith.
God was sovereign, but allowed Satan's choices to be exercised within his plan, to enable his purpose to be achieved.
Satan had to operate within the fence God built — there were clear limits placed on what Satan could and could not do — so that the fence-builder's purpose would reach its designed outcome.

Jonah's Story

Like Job, the story of Jonah is also recorded in the Bible in a book bearing his name — "Jonah".
In a nutshell, God required Jonah to go and preach to the city of Nineveh, the capital city of Assyria.
Jonah was to tell them that unless they changed their ways God would destroy them.

The story of Jonah clearly shows how God acts towards us, not just to Jonah and the city of Nineveh.

It's a great story.
Have you read it lately?
If not, how about putting the book down, run and get your Bible, and read it before you continue reading here.
It's just a short read of four brief chapters.

Or hop onto the net again, point to *Bible Gateway* and type "Jonah" in the Search Box.

The "Book of Jonah" link will come up as the first reference.
Click this link, and the Book of Jonah will be displayed.

Are you back again?
Did you notice how much God was in control and was orchestrating the events in the story?

The word of the Lord came to Jonah ...
Then the Lord sent a great wind on the sea ...
Now the Lord provided a huge fish to swallow Jonah ...
And the Lord commanded the fish ...
Then the word of the Lord came to Jonah a second time ...
God did not bring on them the destruction he had threatened ...
Then the Lord God provided a leafy plant and made it grow ...
God provided a worm ...
God provided a scorching east wind ...

This definitely sounds like the God whom Isaiah describes.

> *I am the Lord, and there is no other; apart from me there is no God.*
> *I will strengthen you, though you have not acknowledged me,*
> *so that from the rising of the sun to the place of its setting people may know there is none besides me.*
> *I am the Lord, and there is no other.*
> *I form the light and create darkness,*
> *I bring prosperity and create disaster;*
> *I, the Lord, do all these things.*
> *[Isaiah 45 : 5 — 7 NIV]*

God's sovereignty is clear, but what about man's limited-freewill?
The Jonah story is a great example that shows the difference between God's sovereignty and man's "freewill".

God had a plan for Jonah to follow.

Jonah chose to disobey and run from God's presence.
Fancy thinking he could do that? He obviously had lost his copy of Psalm 139.

Well, that was his choice and he exercised his will in catching a ship to Tarshish and heading in the opposite direction.

The storm, the potential shipwreck and the fish attack that God arranged eventually got Jonah's attention and he quickly learnt to pray.

When God asked him to go to Nineveh again, he was ready to agree.
Jonah certainly had the ability to make choices and exercise his will, but in the end, God had his way.
Jonah's will was not free, but limited within the overall plan God had for him.

God has a plan for all of us.
We'll discuss this in detail in the next chapter.
We have the authority to exercise our wills and make all the choices we want, but these will only determine the quality of the journey — they can only make the journey wonderful or dangerous.

God has no hesitation in providing trouble, persecutions, even disasters, to get our attention and get us back on track.

Even Jonah in the middle of his troubles and deep sea crisis recognised this fact.
In his prayer, he revealed his understanding of God's grace, and the futility of relegating God and his plans to last place in his life.
He realised that those who pursue selfish ideas and choices miss out on the benefits and blessings of God's love and grace while doing so.

The Bible says we can experience God's kindness and grace or his sternness and correction on the journey — the choice is ours.

But our final destination, the ultimate outcome, has already been chosen by the Sovereign God, who loves us, wants the best for us and will make sure we get it.

Indeed, one way or another, in this age or another, through the lake of fire if need be, God will get us to where he has destined us to be.
Just ask Jonah.

> *Indeed, one way or another, in this age or another, through the lake of fire if need be, God will get us to where he has destined us to be. Just ask Jonah.*

Joseph's Story

The story of Joseph also shows us how ignorant we are about God's workings on this planet.
We rarely understand how resolutely God works at achieving his plans.
We think we make all the decisions in our lives by our "freewill", but we have no idea that God is overseeing the whole production from behind the scenes, from outside the fence.

The best we can say is that we are free to make decisions and choices within the paddock God has assigned to us, to exercise our will within the boundaries of the fence he has put in place.

The Joseph story is another great story worth re-reading, or reading for the first time. But it's a bit longer than Jonah's story, so I'll describe it briefly for you.
(If you're interested to read it yourself, look in the second half of Genesis, the first book in the Bible. Or go to the net and start with Genesis 37 in the Search Box at *Bible Gateway*.)

Joseph's brothers hated him because he was their father's favourite. They hated him even more when he told them his dreams predicted that one day his brothers would be his servants.

Because of their hatred and jealousy, the brothers threw Joseph into a pit intending to kill him, but sold him to passing traders instead. These traders were on their way to Egypt and, on their arrival there, sold Joseph to Potiphar, the captain of Pharaoh's guard.

Through extraordinary circumstances, Joseph became Prime Minister of Egypt, second only to Pharaoh.
In this position, he saved Egypt from ruin during a long famine that Joseph himself had previously predicted.

Because the famine also affected Canaan, where Joseph's family lived, his brothers came to Egypt to buy food from the reserves Joseph had built up during the years before the famine hit.
After several meetings with Joseph, whom they failed to recognise, the brothers finally discovered they were doing business with their own brother, when he revealed his identity to them.

> "I am your brother Joseph, the one you sold into Egypt!
> And now, do not be distressed and do not be angry with yourselves for selling me here, because it was to save lives that God sent me ahead of you." [Genesis 45 : 4 — 5 NIV]

Later, the rest of Joseph's family moved to Egypt where Jacob, his father, subsequently died.

After their father's death, the brothers feared Joseph might now take revenge on them.
However, Joseph assured them that their evil intentions were used by God to achieve his plans to save Jacob and his growing family.

> "You intended to harm me, but God intended it for good to accomplish what is now being done, the saving of many lives."
> [Genesis 50 : 20 NIV]

Sounds a bit like what Jesus might have said to those who put him on the cross, doesn't it?

The J men — Job, Jonah, Joseph — had remarkable stories.
God was really running the show in each case, even when most of those in the show didn't recognise it.
However, the wise King Solomon did.

> "Many are the plans in a person's heart,
> but it is the Lord's purpose that prevails."
> [Proverbs 19 : 21 NIV]

and

> "You may make your plans, but God directs your actions."
> [Proverbs 16 : 9 GNT]

were two of his thoughts on the subject.

God has erected a fence for all of us individually, and for humanity collectively.
He has an overall purpose for everything and everyone he has created, and it will be accomplished regardless of the choices we make on the journey.

So he will not allow us the choice to jump over the fence and miss the final destiny and happiness he has chosen for us to enjoy.

Responsible Parenting

Parenting is an extreme sport.
Parents are always aiming for a better result, risking life, limb and reputation to achieve their best, not for themselves though, but for their kids.
I think parenting is a good example of the Magic Combo we discussed a bit earlier.

Parents need to be the fence-builders, setting the limits and defining the boundaries to keep their kids safe and to give them the freedom and encouragement to grow, explore and enjoy life without exposing them to dangers they are not yet equipped to handle.

I appreciate this sounds good in theory, but it often doesn't work out smoothly.
Problems arise mainly because of the fence.
Children are not taught the meaning or benefit of the fence, nor to respect it (and therefore their parents who erected it).

Equally, parents do not always respect their own fence, or keep it in good repair.
(And, of course, the position of the fence needs to be adjusted periodically as the children grow and mature, until the children can eventually become fence-builders themselves.)

Parents need to exercise their governance role, their sovereignty, with love and consistency, and ensure that their children stay within the boundaries, even when they are determined to break loose.
Even though it may seem unkind, or overly protective, good parents do not allow their children to go outside the boundaries they have planned for their children's well-being.

As a good father, God, in his sovereignty, has built fences around the paddocks he has given us in which to grow, explore and enjoy life.
Because he is love (see Chapter One) his fence-building has only our best interests and safety in mind, like any good parent's does.

Outside the fence is danger on a cosmic scale.
Many of us are determined to ignore God's fences and desire pastures outside the paddocks we have been given.
Regardless of humankind's ignorance, arrogance and rebellion, God will never, never allow us to go there.
This is his sovereign decision, which we will discuss more fully in the next chapter.

In hindsight, I can look back and see God's guiding hand in my life, and the fences I have bumped into in my most arrogant moments.
How about you?
These things were "just meant to be" — people say.
Chance meetings now appear as planned and so beneficial when looking back.
And even if we cannot identify with the experiences of these now, I am certain we all will eventually.
That's part of God's plan too.

The Giant Sudoku

My wife loves solving Sudoku puzzles (and I'm known to enjoy them pretty frequently too).
It occurs to me that these are another example of the Magic Combo we have been discussing.
Each puzzle has a designer and players.

The designer creates the puzzle, determines its end result and sets the rules to be used in its solution.

As such, the designer builds the fence inside which the players must remain to enjoy and solve the puzzle she has created.
The rules are written in negative form (you must *not* have a numeral duplicated in any one row, column or region) as were the rules for the behaviour for the management team in our corporate governance-management model above.

Although there is only one correct solution or end result for each puzzle, players can work towards that in any way they choose — as long as they keep to the rules.
Within these limits, they are free to make a wide range of decisions and use a variety of strategies.

They have "limited freewill". (There's that oxymoron again.)

They can guess, follow clues logically, backtrack, erase the work done so far, start again, or any combination of these. They can even put it aside for a time and come back to it sometime later.

But the correct solution never changes, nor do the rules, no matter what the player does.
The designer is sovereign, and all players must submit to her sovereignty.

	7	8	5		2			
	5				3	7		
8	9				4		3	5
	3	9	5		6			1
4								6
6			7		8	4	9	
1	2		3				5	4
			4	1		3		
			3		8	9	6	

Within the puzzle itself, there are clues to help fill in the blanks and reach the goal.
And there is usually a rescue plan in place for those who can't make it on their own.
If the puzzle is in a book, there might be hints or the final solution in the back.
If the puzzle is attempted online, hints and prompts are readily available with the click of a mouse button.

One way or another, it is possible for every player to achieve the end result, although they may take different routes and different amounts of time.

We happily accept there is only one solution; we happily accept there are rules that cannot be broken; we happily accept the challenge the designer has set before us.
That's just the way things are!

As is life.
God is sovereign, the Designer, who has decided on the end result and set the rules for getting there.

Humankind can make choices and decisions like a Sudoku player, but in the end, there is only one result and the same rules apply to all players.

And thankfully, there is a rescue plan in place for those who can't or won't get to that result during their lifetime on the planet.

Surfing the Big Waves

An illustration that I use to help me explain the choices we have within the sovereign will of God was first shared with me by a friend, and from whom I have learned so much about God's grace, but who disagrees with the thesis of this book.

Interestingly, my friend uses this story to explain how we all have freewill; while I use the same story to show how God's will always prevails in the end, even though we can make individual choices on the way.

Consider a surfer riding the waves on an ocean beach.
He has no control over a wave, it will take him from the deep to the shallows — that is its design and intent.

But while riding a wave, the surfer can make a multitude of choices. He has the freedom to change direction, cut across it, tunnel through it, or whatever.
The surfer has "freewill" to ride the wave, to live life, however he decides.

Most of what my friend says is true.
But he misses at least one vital point.
Regardless of how the surfer cuts and turns, the wave "wins" in the end. The wave takes him from where it picks him up to the shore. Indeed, the wave is vital — without it, he goes nowhere.

If the surfer missed the wave by not being in the right place at the right time or by deciding to back out of the wave or by totally ignoring it rather than riding it, the ocean has another coming along not too far behind.

And they keep coming until the surfer finally gets back to shore.

God has a big wave for all of us.
It takes us from where it finds us into the shore.
We can make many choices over the years we are riding the wave — we can work with it or against it, or back out of it or even ignore it altogether, but eventually one of them will take us home.

> *God has a big wave for all of us.*

And there are many big waves, coming at different times, picking up different surfers along the way, all heading in the same direction and ending up on the same shore, eventually. All surfers end up on the shore in the end.

The Bible describes Jesus as the true light that gives light to everyone or, as paraphrased by me, the wave that gets everyone to the shore.
We'll discuss more about how Jesus does this in Chapter Four.

God is sovereign over his creation, of which we and our earth are integral parts.
The Bible puts it this way:

> *For from him and through him and to him are all things.*
> *[Romans 11 : 36 BV]*

because

> *God works out everything in conformity with the purpose of his will.*
> *[Ephesians 1 : 11 BV]*

With our understanding that God really loves us and that he is in total control of all he has created, we can now consider and appreciate his grand plan. Our next chapter begins to fill in the details of this plan.

CHAPTER 3

God's Awesome Plan

S O what does a God,
who *is* love and who *is* sovereign or Lord of all,
have in store for his creation?

What would a God do — a God who loves perfectly and consistently, and has the authority and power to do whatever he chooses to do? And how could we, small human creatures in a universe of enormous dimensions, possibly know what that might be?

Let's attempt to get a perspective on the scale of these measurements before we go on.

We Are Very Very Small

I am awestruck when I consider the vastness of our universe. Distances in space are so great they are measured in light-years. Miles or kilometres just won't do.

Since we are still discovering parts of the universe, we don't know how much there is still to be found. So we don't really know how big the universe will be when it is all discovered.

But at last count, it seems that the universe is about 15 billion light-years across, and each of those light-years is about 9 trillion km, so that makes our universe very, very big.

For the curious (who can also cope with some arithmetic) ... The speed of light is about 300,000 km/sec, which means light travels 300,000 km every second.
That's about 1 billion km per hour,
   which is about 25 billion km per day,
   which is about 9 trillion km per year.

Numbers like that are too large for us to fathom.
But here's something that might help to get a handle on all of this — a beam of light takes just 1 second to travel 7 times around the Earth.

The universe is dotted with galaxies, about 100 billion of them, that we know of.
One of those galaxies, in the outer suburbs of the universe, is ours, called the Milky Way.
Our solar system is one of the many systems in that galaxy and, our planet, called Earth, is just a small dot in that system.

And you and I are just two of several billion people residing on that small planet.
So, you and I are two small dots residing on a small dot planet which is located in the outer suburbs of one of the 100 billion galaxies in the universe.

As human beings, we sometimes think of ourselves as big shots or VIP's or just plain important.

But as it is so obvious to see, we are very, very small in the grand scheme of things, in God's massive creation.

So isn't it amazing to think that we puny residents of such a small planet in this enormous universe could possibly know what God's plans are?
I can't think of any other circumstances in which the insignificant, "the created", have access to the thinking and planning of the Almighty, "the Creator".

But we do, it's all in the script, although it wasn't always as obvious as it has become to us.

Age-old Secrets

Most of us enjoy a good mystery.
Police and detective stories have been some of the world's best sellers for decades.
And what is the most popular genre of programs on western television channels?
Apart from the recent phenomenon of reality shows, it's police and detective dramas of various shapes and sizes — mysteries.

A well-written mystery, story or drama, releases clues bit by bit as the plot unfolds, and it's not until the end, or very close to the end, that the mystery is solved, the secret hidden from the beginning is fully revealed — who really "done" it.

There are quite a few mysteries or secrets discussed in the Bible. Some were hidden from humankind for generations, some revealed progressively through the ages, and some revealed without warning until they were "dropped" on us.

God's ultimate purpose for his creation was one of these — a secret for ages, although a few clues have been let slip from time to time, beginning several thousand years ago.

Let's see if you can discover God's ultimate plan for us as I sprinkle a trail of clues from Hebrew prophets and authors of past centuries. Are you ready?

One of the first clues I bumped into on my journey of discovering God's plan for us was a statement in a conversation King David had while he was being urged to be reconciled to his estranged son.

> *Like water spilled on the ground, which cannot be recovered, so we must die.*
> *But that is not what God desires; rather, he devises ways so that a banished person does not remain banished from him.*
> *[2 Samuel 14 : 14 NIV]*

Hint: We might be banished or disappear from this planet, but we will not be banished from God. He has plans to keep in touch with us.

This same idea was expressed by the prophet Jeremiah.

> *For no one is cast off by the Lord forever.*
> *Though he brings grief, he will show compassion, so great is his unfailing love.*
> *[Lamentations 3 : 31 — 32 NIV]*

King David himself declared that

> *All the ends of the earth*
> *will remember and turn to the Lord,*
> *and all the families of the nations*
> *will bow down before him,*
> *for dominion belongs to the Lord*
> *and he rules over the nations.*
>
> *All the rich of the earth will feast and worship;*
> *all who go down to the dust will kneel before him —*
> *those who cannot keep themselves alive.*
> *[Psalm 22 : 27 — 29 NIV]*

Hint: Both the affluent and the poor, the alive and the dead, will all worship the Lord.

And reinforced in another of David's psalms.

> *You who answer prayer, to you all people will come.*
> *[Psalm 65 : 2 NIV]*

Hint: Everyone will come to the One who answers prayer.

Are you beginning to discover God's secret?
David let the cat out of the bag with these gems ...

> *All the nations you have made will come and worship before you, Lord; they will bring glory to your name.*
> *[Psalm 86 : 9 NIV]*

> *The Lord is gracious and compassionate, slow to anger and rich in love. The Lord is good to all; he has compassion on all he has made.*
> *[Psalm 145 : 8 – 9 NIV]*

And Isaiah, another of Israel's famous prophets, added his share with these ...

> *On this mountain the Lord Almighty will prepare a feast of rich food for all peoples, a banquet of aged wine — the best of meats and the finest of wines.*
> *On this mountain he will destroy the shroud that enfolds all peoples,*
> *the sheet that covers all nations;*
> *he will swallow up death forever.*
> *The Sovereign Lord will wipe away the tears from all faces;*
> *he will remove his people's disgrace from all the earth.*
> *The Lord has spoken.*
> *[Isaiah 25 : 6 – 8 NIV]*

> *"Turn to me and be saved, all you ends of the earth;*
> *for I am God, and there is no other.*
> *By myself I have sworn,*
> *my mouth has uttered in all integrity a word that*
> *will not be revoked:*
> *Before me every knee will bow;*
> *by me every tongue will swear."*
> *[Isaiah 45 : 22 — 23 NIV]*
>
> *"From one New Moon to another and from one*
> *Sabbath to another,*
> *all mankind will come and bow down before me,"*
> *says the Lord.*
> *[Isaiah 66 : 23 NIV]*

Is it starting to come together?
Here's another significant clue.

Israel's Jubilee

Have you ever read about the jubilee that was celebrated every 50 years in the ancient nation of Israel?

It is a powerful, almost unbelievable, practice in the life of those people, prescribed by God as an essential part of their national life. And it gives us clear understanding of how God wanted his model nation to live, and provides another telling clue to the plan God has in place for all of his creation.

You'll find it described in Leviticus Chapter 25 and mentioned in Leviticus Chapter 27 and Numbers Chapter 36.
If you're interested to see the "original" take a moment to read Leviticus Chapter 25.
Leviticus is the third book in the Bible, or you can read Leviticus on the *Bible Gateway* website *(www.biblegateway.com)*.

Here's my version.
Every fifty years everything was to be restored to the way it originally was — slaves were set free, debts were cancelled, property returned to its original owners.

Our way of living, especially in the western world, is so far removed from what happened there that it is almost impossible for us to understand how such an arrangement would work.

Nevertheless, with the huge amount of debt we all carry, whether as individuals, businesses, governments or nations, and the percentage of our incomes we use to service these debts, surely it is a better way to live — as God's way always is.

If the Jubilee is God's way, and worked so well in the ancient past, don't you think this might be still God's way and can say something to us about how things will pan out for his entire creation in the end?

> **The Jubilee for Israel becomes the pattern for the Jubilee for all of us.**

The physical jubilee that occurred in national Israel says something exciting to me about the spiritual way it will work at the end of time in the universe.

All of humankind is in debt to God and are slaves to sin and Satan. But Jesus paid for all our debts to guarantee a jubilee for all of creation. (see Chapter Four)
And we will be returned to our original position and condition — living in harmony with God as beings in the image of God.

The jubilee for Israel becomes the pattern for the jubilee for all of us. Paul, the champion apostle, describes this jubilee in these words...

> *I consider that our present sufferings are not worth comparing with the glory that will be revealed in us.*

> *For the creation waits in eager expectation for the children of God to be revealed.*
> *For the creation was subjected to frustration, not by its own choice, but by the will of the one who subjected it, in hope that the creation itself will be liberated from its bondage to decay and brought into the freedom and glory of the children of God.*
> *[Romans 8 : 18 — 21 NIV]*

Israel may no longer obey God's commands today, and we certainly don't either.
But when all the kingdoms and governments of this world have become Christ's, God's ways will be followed and Jesus will oversee creation's jubilee.
Isn't the Bible so full of the promise of eventual universal harmony and happiness?

The Secret Fully Revealed

Paul says on several occasions that some of God's secrets, or mysteries as many English Bible translations call them, that had been hidden from previous generations in previous ages, were fully revealed to him.

And he in turn revealed these secrets to those to whom he wrote his letters, and therefore of course, as readers of those letters, to us.
That's why I keep quoting him so often.
He sees the whole picture better than anyone else.

Unfortunately, some people who read the Bible haven't seen these secrets revealed, and are totally in the dark about some of God's most exciting plans.

One of these secrets, the one related to the theme of this book, is God's plan to bring unity to everything in heaven and on earth under Christ.

> *He made known to us the secret of his will according to his good pleasure, which he himself had previously decided, to be put into effect when the times reach their completion — to bring unity to all things in heaven and on earth under Christ.*
> *[Ephesians 1 : 9 – 10 BV]*

And because it includes all, it means Gentiles as well as Jews, which was certainly a surprise to the Jews, God's chosen nation of the Old Testament era.

> *This secret is that through the gospel the Gentiles are joint heirs with Israel, members together of one body, and sharers together in the promise in Christ Jesus.*
> *[Ephesians 3 : 6 BV]*

And because it includes all, it means not-yet-believers as well as believers. Paul explained to his apprentice Timothy

> *That is why we labour and strive, because we have put our hope in the living God, who is the Saviour of all people, and especially of those who believe.*
> *[1 Timothy 4 : 10 NIV]*

after having previously told him that

> *God wills all people to be saved and come to recognise the truth.*
> *[1 Timothy 2 : 4 BV]*

And because it includes all, it means the whole of humankind who has ever lived or ever will live.

> *God was in Christ reconciling the world to himself, not counting people's sins against them.*
> *2 Corinthians 5 : 19 BV]*

And because it includes all, it means the whole universe will also be renewed and restored.

> *the creation itself will be liberated from its bondage to decay and brought into the freedom and glory of the children of God.*
> *[Romans 8 : 21 NIV]*

And because it includes all, it means everyone is reconciled and properly related to God.

> *After everything is under the power of God's Son, he will put himself under the power of God, who put everything under his Son's power. Then God will mean everything to everyone.*
> *[1 Corinthians 15 : 28 CEV]*

What a plan!
A great plan for all of us, no matter who we are, where we live, or how we've lived. (Although *how* we've lived, affects *when* we receive the benefits of the plan.)
And it's no longer a secret.
It was fully revealed almost 2000 years ago.

Was this a surprise to you?
It certainly would be if you belong to some of the churches in your city, or listen to people who do.
It's definitely *not* what is generally taught in their pulpits, or discussed in their Bible study groups, or announced in their evangelistic campaigns.

Although it *is* what they seem to say at most of their funeral services, but I'll leave that discussion until Chapter Five.

The approach of some Christians to this great news, if it is ever discovered at all, is a bit like Jonah's when he discovered that God had forgiven the city of Nineveh.
He was furious when he discovered that God would forgive that pagan city, although he never criticised the way God continually forgave the chosen nation of Israel that he belonged to.

How dare God treat pagans the same way he treats us!
We are the chosen!
We worship God, and serve him and offer sacrifices to him.
We have the Scriptures and the patriarchs and the prophets.
We are special.

Some Christians are similarly aghast that God will allow all who have not gotten themselves right with God during their lifetime on this planet, as they have, to be reconciled to him later.
"How unfair is that?" they argue.
And they don't mind saying so quite publicly.
So what is God's purpose, in simple point form?

◊ To head up the universe under his Son, Jesus Christ.
◊ To reconcile the universe to himself.
◊ To become everything to everyone.

In other words, God is going to use Jesus Christ to bring all the universe into unity and harmony with himself.
And this has been God's plan, in his script, from the very beginning — even from before time began — the Bible reveals.

The Natural Rhythm of the Surf Beach

Let's return to the surf beach we visited towards the end of the previous chapter as we explore the wonder of God's plan here.
Australia has superb surfing beaches, and some of them, like Bells Beach, have become internationally famous for world championships.

As well as the excitement of riding the white caps to shore, there is also the danger of the undertow or rip lurking beneath them.
So lifesavers patrol our beaches, mark the safest sections in which to swim and surf, and stand ready to save any who ignore the markings, become injured or fall victim to the outgoing undertow.

For me, the beach, with its waves, undertow, surfers and lifesavers, forms a neat picture of God's purpose to bring all of his creation to unity under the leadership of Jesus Christ.

My wife and I often have a picnic meal on the headland overlooking the main beach at Torquay, not far from Bells Beach.
The water below is dotted with surfers on their boards, having left the shore some time earlier.
Some are on the way in, some are sitting waiting for a good wave, some are just enjoying the view, some are paddling around, some are even heading out toward the open sea.

But eventually, at the end of the day, all of them have returned to the beach.
There are no options in the game plan. All go out to sea and all come back to shore.

As we watch we notice ...
Some surfers immediately catch their wave and come straight to shore.
Some choose to ride their wave more adventurously — changing direction, even going backwards at times, through the tube, up on the crest, lost in the foam, but eventually arriving "home".
Others fall from their wave or miss it altogether and have to wait for another.

Regardless of the variety of manoeuvres or choices made by each surfer, the waves continue to travel towards the shore and all surfers eventually arrive there too.
The natural rhythm of the ocean, the unchanging laws of nature, guarantee it!

So how does this picture demonstrate God's purpose in the world to me?
The surf is the world.
The beach is home, the final destination of every person in the world.

The surfers are God's offspring, scattered all over the world.
Some catch waves early, others take longer having missed waves or not been in the right place at the right time.

God's unchanging purpose for all of his creation is to bring everyone home.
We can't avoid it.
It's the natural rhythm of the universe.

Regardless of the choices we make, the number of waves we miss or ignore or fall from, eventually one of them will bring us to shore.
The surf beach reminds me of God's wonderful plan.

A Huge Project That Will Take Ages to Complete

But can you imagine the size of that project?
Wow! Just as well you and I are not responsible for making it happen!
Just think of the state this planet is in.

I know I have said how very, very small we and our planet are, but you don't have to live on it for long before you realise what a job it will be to bring peace, harmony and happiness to all of us.
Remember the evidence of this we discussed at the beginning of the last chapter?

> *God's unchanging purpose for all of his creation is to bring everyone home.*
> *We can't avoid it.*
> *It's the natural rhythm of the universe.*

And worse still ...
The number of people who will have nothing to do with God or Jesus Christ, together with the number who haven't even heard of Jesus, is increasing as the earth's population soars.

If we add to those numbers the millions who have belonged to these "unreconciled" groups in the past and the billions who will belong to those groups in the future, it's tempting to believe that the task of achieving God's purpose might be an impossible one.

How many people in your street are already reconciled to God through Jesus Christ?
How many in your school or university or workplace?
How many in your town or suburb?

There's still a long, long way to go if your answers to those questions are the same as mine.
But let's remember that God is Sovereign.
He is all powerful.
He will achieve whatever he wants to.

What might seem impossible to us, is definitely possible, indeed easy, for him.

When Jesus' first disciples were thinking about the impossibility of such a task, Jesus reminded them that things as big as this are certainly impossible for us to achieve, but entirely possible with the sovereign God in the driver's seat.

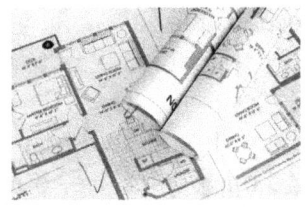

We shall discuss *how* God will achieve his purpose in Chapters Four and Five.
But regardless of how God will achieve his purpose, it is obvious that he will need to be working on his plans over a long period of time, certainly a much longer time than any one of us spends on this planet.

Most of us aren't even brought to harmony with God during our lifetimes, let alone recognise and submit to the Lordship of Jesus Christ during those few years.
So it's going to take God ages to bring this about.

And that's exactly the timespan God has planned to use — it's all included in the script for the Grand Stage Production.

He had this plan before the beginning of time to demonstrate his love and sovereignty and grace, so he created time and the ages, and all their heavenly and earthly components, to implement it. Almost like an inventor who, having a bright idea, went about creating a workshop or laboratory, with all its necessary equipment and tools, in which to design and give expression to his new marvel.

God will achieve his purpose over the course of time, having begun in an age previous to ours and will continue and complete it through this age and other ages that are still future to ours.

Although "ages" is quite long enough, thank you very much, several popular English translations of the New Testament in the Bible make it even longer.
They wrongly translate the original Greek word for ages as eternity, and the Greek word for age-lasting as ever-lasting or eternal, saying that God will take an eternity to achieve his purpose.

In casual English conversation, saying something will take an eternity to happen is considered much the same as taking ages to happen.
"I waited for him for ages" is much the same as "I waited an eternity for him".

But when talking about things on God's scale of measurement, an age, which has a beginning and an end, is definitely not the same as eternity, which has neither beginning nor end.

Indeed eternity is not related to time at all — it is time-less.
God is eternal, he resides in eternity, he is timeless, everything where he lives just *is*.
That is so hard for us earth-and-time-bound creatures to understand. God created time just for us, so that everything that is doesn't happen all at once for us.

When Paul is describing a part of God's plan to the New Testament churches, he mentions that God will take ages to raise everyone to life through Christ, but not an eternity.
It won't be completed until the ages or the times have been completed.

> *He made known to us the secret of his will according to his good pleasure, which he himself had previously decided, to be put into effect when the times reach their completion — to bring unity to all things in heaven and on earth under Christ.*
> *[Ephesians 1 : 9, 10 BV]*

Some of us are restored during the ages, and the remainder at their end when Jesus hands his completed kingdom over to God the Father, so God can be everything to everyone, as God has decided and scripted he will be.

The Best Exotic Marigold Hotel

At the risk of trivialising this great plan of God's, and his overwhelming commitment and sovereign power to achieve it, let me refer to a comedy I enjoyed recently, called *The Best Exotic Marigold Hotel*.

The movie tells the story of a group of misfit British pensioners who were enticed to retire at an exotic hotel resort in India by a glossy travel brochure.

On arrival, the hotel was discovered to be dilapidated and in very poor repair, hardly even habitable, let alone offering resort accommodation and style — nothing like its advertised appearance and description.

Each time the newly arrived residents complained about some deficiency in the building or its facilities, the young Indian manager of the hotel would respond with something like,

"Everything will be all right in the end. So if it's not all right, then it is not yet the end."

That line resonated with me as a humorous, visual reminder of God's plan to reconcile all of creation to himself in the end, even though the world is still in such a dilapidated and violent state in the present.
Since all are not yet reconciled to God, we are definitely not at the end, because "everything will be all right in the end".

God still has the remainder of this age, and more ages to come, in which to complete his mission. But complete it he will, or the Saviour of the world will have wasted his time.

So, with the same optimism as the hotel manager, but with the guaranteed assurance of success, eventually, at the conclusion of the ages, at the end of time, God will have achieved his purpose — in full.
He will have demonstrated his love, power and grace through Jesus Christ and everything and everyone will be reconciled to God.

> **Everything will be all right in the end. So if it's not all right, then it's not yet the end.**

A few weeks after the death and resurrection of Jesus, Peter and John healed a lame beggar at the temple gate in Jerusalem.
Crowds rushed to the scene of the miracle, so Peter used the opportunity to give credit to Jesus for the healing and to teach the gathering crowd about God's plan to use Jesus to bring spiritual healing to them, and eventually to the world.

In this conversation, Peter said that Jesus, who had by this time returned to his Father in heaven, would remain there (in heaven) until the time came for God to begin restoring everything.

> *He must remain in heaven until the time comes for*
> *all things to be made new, as God announced through*
> *his holy prophets of long ago.*
> *[Acts 3 : 21 GNT]*

So it's all going to happen ... and it starts on Jesus' return.
Or using the way Peter expressed it to the crowd at the temple gate, Jesus was not going to return from heaven until it was time for God to start restoring everything.
The two come together, whichever way you look at it.

Isn't that really good news?
God has a plan to bring everything and everyone in the universe into harmony and unity under the Lordship of his Son, Jesus Christ.

And this will be completed at the end of the ages so that we can all step into eternity together, into the timeless realm in which God lives.

Knowing God

So how is it that so few are aware of this wonderful plan?
There are many reasons, but most of them require discussions that go well beyond the theme of this book, which is to present, in lay person's terms, the good news about God and his plan for us, the pinnacle of his creation.

But two of these reasons can be mentioned briefly here.
Firstly, most people don't know God as a God of love and sovereignty.
If you've been reading this book sequentially, and the Bible verses referenced, you probably do.
Most people think of God as a mean, angry, easily upset, vengeful tyrant who will make people pay for all the wrongs they have committed with ever-lasting torment in a fiery place they call hell.

But when we know the truth about God's character, it seems impossible to believe that God doesn't have a plan which ensures his entire family will be in a loving harmonious relationship with him and all other family members at the end of time.

The second reason is that most people don't know the end of the story.
And this stems from the way some people read their Bibles.
The Bible is not one single book telling a continuous story from beginning to end.

It is a collection of many books — histories, letters, poems, and prophecies — that God inspired their many authors to write over hundreds of years.
These describe God's dealings with nations, churches and individuals as he implements his plan for achieving his purposes.

Although an approximate chronology can be assumed from the first book (Genesis) to the last (The Revelation), an exact sequence can not.

Genesis is certainly the beginning; but whatever we make of the details of The Revelation, it is not the end of the story, as many people presume.

Its closing chapters do offer a description of the final age, with a burning lake of fire, Jesus Christ on a royal throne ruling with those already reconciled to God sharing in his government, and with those still unreconciled outside the heavenly city. And this is where most people stop, believing this to be the end result.

But, the final age is not the end !

And it is within Paul's writings that we discover what happens *after* the ages are completed — information that was revealed to him and not revealed to John, the author of The Revelation.

> *For as in Adam all die, so in Christ all will be made alive.*
> *But each in turn: Christ the firstfruits; then, when he comes, those who belong to him.*
> *Then the end will come, when he hands over the kingdom to God the Father after he has destroyed all dominion, authority and power.*
> *For he must reign until he has put all his enemies under his feet.*
> *The last enemy to be destroyed is death.*
> *For he has put everything under his feet.*
> *Now when it says that "everything" has been put under him, it is clear that this does not include God himself, who put everything under Christ.*
> *When he has done this, then the Son himself will be made subject to him who put everything under him, so that God may be all in all.*
> *[1 Corinthians 15 : 22 — 28 NIV]*

Clearly, if we're looking for the end of the story, 1 Corinthians 15 is more likely.
God will be everything to everyone after the ages have concluded, as we all move into eternity.

Paul describes a picture of a perfect spiritual realm, with no sin, no corruption, no rebellion, no death, no lake of fire, no authority other than God's, and everyone reconciled to God living happily under him.

Wouldn't that be the end result
    for a God of love (Chapter One)
    who wants everyone to be saved (1 Timothy 2 : 4)
    and has the power to achieve whatever he wants (Chapter Two)?

Surely, we can expect nothing less than a plan that produces the greatest good for humankind and majestic glory and universal applause for the Creator.

In many ways, this chapter is the climax of the book.
Arriving here is a bit like standing on the summit of a mountain.
The rest of the countryside is all visible from here, and can be seen in true perspective.

In this chapter, we have seen the grand plan God has designed to demonstrate his character and to bring happiness and harmony to the whole of his creation.

Looking backwards to Chapters One and Two we can see those aspects of God's character, his love and sovereignty, which define and motivate his dealings with us and underscore his plan.

Looking forwards to Chapters Four and Five we will see how God's love and sovereignty enables his plan to be successfully carried out.

So let's move to Chapter Four to see how God's love, expressed through his Son, Jesus Christ, kicks this off.

CHAPTER 4

God's Champion Lifesaver

THE sandwich board sign on the footpath grabbed my attention.
"Geelong Woman Saved" it announced in bold arresting typeface.
The sign outside the local newsagent was advertising the main news story in that day's Geelong newspaper.
It was Thursday 24th Feb 2011, and my thoughts began running across the situations that could have prompted such a headline.

Where was she and what was she saved from?
There were severe floods in several states of Australia — Victoria, New South Wales, Western Australia, and Queensland — at that time.
There was a cyclone crossing the coast in Queensland, and bush fires in Western Australia and Victoria.
And a recent house fire in Geelong.
All these happened in the recent past and could have been the context of the story the headlines were referring to.

But no, it was none of these.
It was the devastating earthquake in Christchurch, New Zealand.

This woman, from Geelong, Australia, but on holiday in New Zealand, was in a building that had been severely damaged in the earthquake and had been rescued several hours after emergency teams began inspecting mangled buildings looking for possible survivors.
She had been saved from death in an earthquake-stricken building "across the ditch".

Knowing the context of the newspaper headline would have helped me understand more than the sandwich board headline.

Context, Context, Context

In the real estate industry, it is said there are three vital ingredients necessary for making wise investment decisions — "location, location, location".
In story-telling of any sort, they become "context, context, context".
And this is particularly true when discussing Bible topics.

The context is vital if we are to understand what "being saved" means.
The news that "he saved the day" immediately begs a question asking for more information.
"She saved my bacon" and "it saved me heaps" do the same.

A person who has a terrible illness is saved when a new drug or procedure that cures their disease becomes available.

Interestingly, in several cases of illness and healing in the New Testament of the Bible, where the Greek word "saved" is used to describe the final state of a previously ill person, most translators use their contextual judgement and proclaim them "healed" rather than "saved", even though "saved" is the literal translation of the Greek word used.

At most other times, "saved" is correctly and literally translated, and we are left to make the judgement as to what those involved have been saved from.
We need to examine the context of the story for ourselves.

The Story in a Nutshell

God originally created humankind in his own likeness.

He did this to produce an extension of his divine family that would govern the earth for him.
This adventure began with Adam, and his wife Eve, in the Garden of Eden.
You can read about their story in the early chapters of Genesis, the first book in the Bible.

Although the Garden was a perfect, heavenly paradise, it provided a very sheltered life for Adam and Eve.
They could "only" experience the peace and joy of living in harmony with God under his loving care and provision.
They had no idea what the full scope of life on earth had the potential to offer.
They certainly were not aware of how well off they were as they had nothing with which to compare their idyllic lifestyle.

God provided a tree of the knowledge of good and evil in the middle of the Garden knowing that given the choice, Adam and Eve would want to experience its "benefits".
God told them to avoid this tree, so when they did touch it, their disobedience automatically triggered the loss of their intimate, dependent relationship with him.
God referred to this loss as "death".

Being assigned to death in this way gave Adam and Eve the opportunity to experience aspects of the character of God they hadn't yet seen.
They could now know God as a lover of sinners, not just saints, and experience the discipline, grace and forgiveness of a loving Father toward wayward humanity.

They were subsequently removed from their Garden Paradise and given the challenging task of negotiating the outside world of good and evil, and providing their own food, shelter and creature comforts.

In that separated state in the outside world, Adam and Eve gave birth to our "fallen" human race.
Consequently, all of us have been born into this world separated from God and with a likeness to God that is barely recognisable any more, and with little or no interest in governing God's earth for him or for his benefit.

So we all start out experiencing life without knowing God, serving our own interests and governing our own little worlds to serve our own selfish ambitions.

Because God planned for this to happen, he also planned to bring it back into order and have his original purpose and plans achieved.
God's plan, designed before the world even began, was to save us from death, our God-separatedness, and from our inherited Adam-likeness.
This saving would restore us to our intimate, dependent relationship with God and to our original state of God-likeness.

And Jesus Christ, God's Son, was and is the key to both of these restoration projects, as we shall see in the next few pages.
But before we do, let's explore the meanings of some of the words that are frequently used when people speak about God, Jesus, the Garden of Eden and the Bible in general.

What is Death?

Death is a separation, not the end, as we have been conditioned to believe.
It is just one event in our life's journey.

When we die physically, we are separated from our bodies, from our family and friends, from life on this planet.
So, physical death is a separation from our physical body and our physical world.

As we have already seen, spiritual death, the death introduced in the Garden, is also a separation.
It is a separation from intimacy with God, the One who made us, and a separation from the God-likeness in which humankind was originally created.

Consequently, every person born from that time, as a descendent of the estranged Adam and Eve, has been born in the same condition as Adam and Eve — physically alive (of course) but spiritually dead.

> **Death is a separation, not the end.**

The only exception to this was the extraordinary birth of Jesus Christ, who was not conceived in the normal way, but was the Son of God miraculously implanted into the womb of a young Jewish virgin about 2000 years ago.
So, except for Jesus, we all start off spiritually dead, with no intimate, personal relationship with God, and begin life making our own decisions about right and wrong.

Interestingly, these two deaths are connected.
The spiritual death which caused Adam and Eve to lose their God-likeness meant they also lost their God-like characteristics, like their immortality.

Losing their immortality meant they became mortal, no longer able to live forever.
In fact, one of the reasons God removed them from the Garden was so they could not eat from its tree of life, and live forever in their estranged, rebellious state.

Adam and Eve physically died some time after they left the Garden, so we too are destined to die physically.
Physical death is an automatic consequence of spiritual death, another part of our inherited Adam-likeness.

What is Life?

Stating the obvious, life is the opposite of death.
To have life, to be fully alive, has two aspects that match the two aspects of death.

The first is to be restored to our original position, living in harmony with our Creator, and the second is to be restored to our original condition of God-likeness.
And just as there are two aspects to life, position and condition, so there are two stages of receiving this life, one for each aspect.

The two aspects of spiritual life and death can be illustrated by something more familiar to us — physical life and death.
Suppose you have a friend who dies of a serious illness.
And you have the power to do absolutely anything for your friend.
What would you do?
Suppose you choose to raise your friend to life.
What would be the result?
Your friend would be alive, but still seriously ill, and so would die again.
Not the best result.

Let's start again.
Suppose this time you choose to heal your dead friend.

What would be the result this time?
Your friend would be well, but still dead.
You'd have a healthy dead person on your hands.

Clearly, the best choice would be to heal your friend *and* bring your friend back to life.
Only then would you have a living, healthy friend again.
Two things need to be done for your friend, not one.
He needs to be restored to his original position (alive) and to his original condition (healthy).

We will discuss the first of these restorations shortly in this chapter, and the second in later chapters, beginning with Chapter Five.

What is Sin?

When Adam and Eve decided to live independently of God's design and direction, the Bible says that they sinned, or committed sin.
Our English word "sin" is a translation of the Greek word in the Bible that literally means "miss the mark" or "miss the target".

Adam and Eve were made in God's likeness and designed to live as he does and in perfect harmony with him and his ways.
When they sinned, they missed this target, and had to live a sub-standard or second-rate life.

The Bible is full of stories of people who lived second-rate lives.
Even God's specially chosen nation, Israel, did so.
They were chosen to be a model nation for all other nations, and model citizens for all of the world's citizens — but they blew it too.

Nevertheless, although God's standards were high and impossible to achieve without an intimate relationship with God, there were some stand-outs in the historical records in the Bible.
People like Abraham, King David, Joseph, Hosea, and the first century apostles Peter and Paul.

Even though many of these champions made some horrible mistakes, committed gross sins, they regretted them and asked God for his forgiveness and to restore their relationship with him.
King David, who was one of the worst "target-missers" of all time, was even described by God as a man after his own heart.

But for most of us, it has not been that way.
Many of the world's population have no regard for God, even if they are aware of his existence.
And for those who do, the standards are just too high or too inconvenient or too irrelevant to their lifestyles to be bothered about.

Earthlings of all generations can't even see the target, let alone take aim when they do.
Sadly, we all live a long way from the Garden.
We could well be described as the "walking dead".

Jesus Restores Our Position

So some interesting questions are worth considering.
How could so many, in such a hopeless death state, ever be saved from it?
How could anyone be restored to their original relationship position with God?
And how could we regain our original God-like condition?
How can God achieve his long-term goal that we discussed in the last chapter, the great finale of God's "grand stage production"?

Jesus solves the position problem and God's judgement and rehabilitation program solves the condition problem.
We'll discuss the position solution now, and the condition solution in later chapters.

The miraculously-conceived Jesus Christ, God's Son, has already solved the position problem for all of us.

Jesus came to this planet to save us from death, the separation and independence from God that we inherited from Adam and Eve.
He came to restore us to the original position God created us to have.

How can we know this?
The same source that told us we have a problem also tells us we have a solution.
The same Bible that tells us we are sinners informs us that Jesus paid for our sin.
The Apostle Paul said to the Christians in Corinth ...

> *For I passed on to you the most important things: that Christ died for our sins according to the Scriptures, that he was buried, that he was raised on the third day according to the Scriptures, and that he appeared to Peter, and then to the Twelve.*
> *[1 Corinthians 15 : 3 — 5 BV]*

Peter himself confirmed this statement of Paul's in his letter of encouragement to persecuted Christians in the first century.

> *He [Christ] carried our sins in his body on the cross, so that we might die to sins and live for righteousness; "by his wounds you have been healed".*
> *[1 Peter 2 : 24 BV]*

When John the Baptist was baptising people in the Jordan River and saw Jesus approaching him he shouted to the gathering crowd, "Look, the Lamb of God, who takes away the sin of the world."

Jesus came to restore us to the original position God created us to have.

I'm sure John had no idea how Jesus was going to achieve this.
In fact, he did not live long enough to see much more of Jesus' life, let alone witness his death and resurrection.

He didn't even hear Jesus announce his plans for taking away the sin of the world, because King Herod had John murdered.
John also missed Jesus talking to his disciples about the way he would eventually die, and assuring them that after his death he would draw all people to himself.

> "And I, when I am lifted up from the earth, will draw all people to myself."
> He said this to show the kind of death he was going to die.
> [John 12 : 32 – 33 NIV]

This sounds pretty offensive to some people, especially to those who think we all have free will.
"What, you tell me I'm not going to have any choice in this matter? I'm going to be saved whether I want to be or not? I'm going to enjoy God and all he has for me forever, whether I like that idea or not?"
Yes, we all are.
That's what God's script says.

Our English Bibles don't really help us appreciate the full force of Jesus' statement here.
The original Greek, from which this part of our Bibles is translated, uses a word that more accurately means "drag" rather than "draw". So Jesus was saying that he would literally "drag" all people to himself.

Notice, I'm not saying that. Jesus is.
He'll do whatever it takes to drag people from harm and save them. Even if that means them kicking and screaming all the way.

The Lifesaver on the Beach

The surf beach of previous chapters, describing the natural, unchangeable rhythm of the oceans, helps me see the natural, unchangeable plan of God in the universe.

That plan is to bring all of us — all people of all generations — home to the shore, on one wave or another.

Looking at the state of our world might be prompting you to pose the obvious question, "Do you really mean all of us?"
What about the surfer who is injured, or the one who becomes exhausted, or the one who is captured by the rip and driven out beyond the waves, or the millions who just never see a wave in their lifetime and remain stranded at sea?

That's where the lifesaver comes to the rescue.
He brings to shore those who can't or won't get there themselves.

That's what he's there for.
Sometimes the lifesaver has to battle with them, even subdue and overcome them, to get them to the beach — but that he does.

In God's world, the lifesaver on the beach is Jesus.
He is watching with great interest and compassion as his creation rides the waves and battles the rips of the world.
He describes this aspect of his role in the parables about the lost sheep and lost coin that are recorded in the Bible in Luke Chapter 15.

The sheep and coin that are lost, with no hope of returning home under their own steam, are rescued by their owners.
Jesus' promise that he would even "drag" people to himself, wrestle with them, subdue them if necessary, to get them home would resonate with the experiences of many of our beach lifesavers each summer.

The Bible assures me that no-one will drown while Jesus is on duty in the lifesaver's station!

All of God's creation get home one way or the other, some early in the day, some much later.

And, if you're a parent, you will understand exactly how this works. You give your kids certain freedoms and opportunities to make choices to learn many of life's lessons by personal experience.
But there are some choices you don't allow them.

You don't allow your kids to run onto a busy highway with cars, trucks and other vehicles galloping along in both directions at 100 km per hour at peak hour to learn about the dangers of running onto a busy road.
Your child might be running headlong toward the highway, taking no notice of your previous advice, taking no notice of your frantic screaming, finally being restrained by the strength of your dragging her out of harm's way.

The child is now re-positioned, reconnected, with the parent, no longer separated from him.

> *All of God's creation get home one way or the other, some early in the day, some much later.*

But there's more to consider.
She might have been saved from the immediate danger of the busy highway traffic, but was she saved from her independent, rebellious attitude or condition?
Will she be grateful, see things the parent's way, be ready to act any differently next time?
Not necessarily — some children do; some don't — not at the time anyway.

Would a loving parent do anything less than exert their will by force? Against their child's will? You bet!
Kids just don't have the freedom to choose under these circumstances — if a parent is available to have any say in the matter.

And Jesus does have a say in the matter for every person he has created — and has the presence and power to curtail everyone's freedom to make choices that have fatal consequences.

Interestingly, two great Christian authors, C.S. Lewis and Phillip Yancey, both describe their journey to a relationship with God and their entrance into the kingdom of God as ones characterised by their kicking and screaming all the way.

Everyone Will Meet Jesus One Day

We will all meet the resurrected Jesus at some point in our journey towards eternity.
It may be early in our lifetime here, some time later, or even after this life has concluded.
But it will happen.

And meeting Jesus is a life-changing experience.
It certainly was for me and for every genuine follower of Jesus I know.
The original disciples first met Jesus before his death and resurrection, and that was life-changing enough.

> *As Jesus walked along the shore of Lake Galilee, he saw two brothers who were fishermen, Simon (called Peter) and his brother Andrew, catching fish in the lake with a net. Jesus said to them, "Come with me, and I will teach you to catch people." At once they left their nets and went with him.*
>
> *He went on and saw two other brothers, James and John, the sons of Zebedee. They were in their boat with their father Zebedee, getting their nets ready. Jesus called them, and at once they left the boat and their father, and went with him.*
> *[Matthew 4 : 18 — 22 GNT]*

But when the first century disciples met the resurrected Jesus, even greater changes occurred.

Here is the experience of Thomas, as recorded by John, in which he immediately became aware of the divinity and Lordship of Jesus.

> But Thomas, sometimes called the Twin, one of the Twelve, was not with them when Jesus came.
> The other disciples told him, "We saw the Master."
> But he said, "Unless I see the nail holes in his hands, put my finger in the nail holes, and stick my hand in his side, I won't believe it."
>
> Eight days later, his disciples were again in the room. This time Thomas was with them. Jesus came through the locked doors, stood among them, and said, "Peace to you."
> Then he focused his attention on Thomas. "Take your finger and examine my hands. Take your hand and stick it in my side. Don't be unbelieving. Believe."
> Thomas said, "My Master! My God!"
> [John 20 : 24 – 28 TM]

Saul, the man who subsequently became the famous apostle Paul, had an amazing meeting with the resurrected Jesus while he was on a mission to destroy the followers of Jesus in a neighbouring city. Not only did he meet Jesus, but he was changed from being a hostile opponent to one of the most effective and enthusiastic ambassadors for Jesus and his message in the first century.

> Saul kept on threatening to kill the Lord's followers. He even went to the high priest and asked for letters to the Jewish leaders in Damascus. He did this because he wanted to arrest and take to Jerusalem any man or woman who had accepted the Lord's Way.
>
> When Saul had almost reached Damascus, a bright light from heaven suddenly flashed around him. He fell to the ground and heard a voice that said, "Saul!

Saul! Why are you so cruel to me?"
"Who are you?" Saul asked.
"I am Jesus," the Lord answered. "I am the one you are so cruel to. Now get up and go into the city, where you will be told what to do."

The men with Saul stood there speechless. They had heard the voice, but they had not seen anyone. Saul got up from the ground, and when he opened his eyes, he could not see a thing. Someone then led him by the hand to Damascus, and for three days he was blind and did not eat or drink.

A follower named Ananias lived in Damascus, and the Lord spoke to him in a vision. Ananias answered, "Lord, here I am." The Lord said to him, "Get up and go to the house of Judas on Straight Street. When you get there, you will find a man named Saul from the city of Tarsus. Saul is praying, and he has seen a vision. He saw a man named Ananias coming to him and putting his hands on him, so that he could see again."

Ananias replied, "Lord, a lot of people have told me about the terrible things this man has done to your followers in Jerusalem. Now the chief priests have given him the power to come here and arrest anyone who worships in your name."

The Lord said to Ananias, "Go! I have chosen him to tell foreigners, kings, and the people of Israel about me. I will show him how much he must suffer for worshipping in my name."

Ananias left and went into the house where Saul was staying. Ananias placed his hands on him and said, "Saul, the Lord Jesus has sent me. He is the same one who appeared to you along the road. He wants you to be able to see and to be filled with the Holy Spirit."

> *Suddenly something like fish scales fell from Saul's eyes, and he could see. He got up and was baptised. Then he ate and felt much better. For several days Saul stayed with the Lord's followers in Damascus. Soon he went to the Jewish meeting places and started telling people that Jesus is the Son of God.*
> *[Acts 9 : 1 — 20 CEV]*

In the twenty centuries since, millions of people have experienced similar meetings with Jesus — some more and some less dramatic than those of Thomas and Saul — but meetings that have changed their lives and their view of the future.
They too have become followers of Christ and have served him in various capacities from that time on.

There are many others however, billions in fact, who have not had or will not have this experience during their lifetimes on this planet, but will meet Jesus sitting on his throne sometime in their future. Paul told the first century church in Rome, Corinth and Philippi about this meeting.

> *For we will all stand before the judgement seat of Christ. It is written: "'As surely as I live,' says the Lord, 'every knee will bow before me; every tongue will acknowledge God.'*
> *[Romans 14 : 10 — 11 BV]*

> *For we must all appear before the judgement seat of Christ, so that each of us may receive what is due us*
>
> *for the things done while in the body, whether good or bad.*
> *[2 Corinthians 5 : 10 NIV]*

> *Therefore God exalted him [Jesus] to the highest place and gave him the name that is above every name, that at the name of Jesus every knee should bow, in heaven and on earth and under the earth,*

> *and every tongue acknowledge that Jesus Christ is*
> *Lord, to the glory of God the Father.*
> *[Philippians 2 : 9 — 11 BV]*

Can you imagine the scene?
Before the throne of King Jesus, the Judge, are summoned those who don't know him or have rejected him, even cursed him, in their lifetimes on earth.
Can you imagine the mix of feelings — surprise, wonder, apprehension, fear, even terror — spreading through the crowd?

What do you think happens here?
This throne meeting with Jesus is about the most misunderstood event that is described in the Bible.
Many Christians have been taught that its purpose is the exact opposite of what it really is, and do not understand how the Great White Throne meeting with Jesus for not-yet-believers helps to complete God's loving purpose for the world.

Chapter Five will reveal how.
If you're a Christian who has only been exposed to traditional teaching on this subject, prepare to be surprised.
But just a quick glimpse to keep you from jumping to the next chapter before you finish this one.

Jesus stands and identifies himself.
He explains that he is the Son of God, the babe of Bethlehem, the Christ on the cross, who is not only their judge, but has already paid the penalty for their sin in full.

I can imagine there will be a tumultuous Thomas-like chorus of "My Master! My God!" as waves of relief and gratitude waft through the crowd.

God's Spirit at Work

How will they come to that decision?
    How did Thomas come to his?
    How did Saul (Paul) come to his?
    How did I come to mine?

God reveals himself to us through the work of the Holy Spirit. We don't wake up one day and say, "I think I will believe in God today." We can't just decide to believe in Jesus of our own accord.
The Creator must reveal himself to his creatures.

Jesus said that no-one can come to him unless the Father draws them, and Paul said that no-one could recognise and acknowledge Jesus as Lord unless directed by the Holy Spirit.
All revelation and belief is instigated by God.

It may be that this is happening to you right now.
As you are reading these pages, God may be revealing to you his love and the provision he has made for your sin through the death and resurrection of Jesus Christ, and building a desire in you to not be separated from him any longer.
If so, go with the flow, enjoy being drawn by him.

And it's going to happen for all of us at some stage.
The question is not, *"Will* this person or that person believe in God and Jesus?" but *"When* will this person do so?"
In their time here on this planet, or sometime in their future elsewhere?

It is what Jesus has achieved for us on the cross that saves, not our acceptance of that achievement.
Our acceptance is merely an acknowledgement of the fact.
My understanding is this:
We do not believe so we can be saved; we believe because God has revealed himself and his completed work of salvation to us.

Some churches produce lists of requirements that people have to meet in order to be re-positioned with God, to be saved from their separation from him.
I suggest having another look at the story of Saul's transformation from being an enemy of Christ to being one of his most outspoken supporters and advocates. (just a few pages back)
Done that?
Now reflect on these questions ...

How did God make this great transformation in Saul?

>   Did he use force and power?
>   What was Saul asked to do to help achieve the change?
>   Did Saul have to become pure or holy or sin-free first?
>   Did Saul have to confess his sin first?
>   Did Saul have to first ask for forgiveness?
>   Was it necessary for Saul to be baptised first?
>   Did Saul first have to make good for all he had done wrong?
>   Was Saul invited or advised to accept Jesus as his Saviour?

It was Jesus who came to Saul in a way that could not be ignored, to declare who he was, and to give Saul his marching orders.
Saul, who was later known as Paul, became an instant believer!
He had been chosen — captured might be a better description.
He had been introduced to Jesus Christ, the Saviour of the world, and his past atrocities and opposition to the gospel were no longer an issue.

All that was left for him to do was decide whether he would serve Jesus and follow his instructions or stay dumb-struck and blind in the middle of the road.

If you are, or have been, a church-goer, you may have been present at a meeting where a version of the good news was presented and not-yet-believers were then invited, sometimes strongly so, to become a believer and be saved.

This invitation may have included not only some good news, but some bad news of what the speaker believed would happen if listeners refused, or even delayed accepting, his offer.
Fear, guilt, urgency, and eternal punishment may have been the wheels of the vehicle carrying the "good news" message.

I know this happens in many circles, because I have been guilty of doing this in my younger, less informed days.
Maybe you can remember such salvation appeals or invitations and fear-filled scare tactics.

But I'm guessing you haven't heard an invitation like this one.

> God is on your side. He loves you and holds
> nothing against you.
> If you've never done this before ...
> I invite you to come forward and thank God for
> his goodness and love.

Just in case someone gets upset about such a kind invitation, you might share with them Paul's reminder to the Christians in Corinth that

> God was in Christ reconciling the world to himself,
> not counting people's sins against them.
> [2 Corinthians 5 : 19 BV]

And what did he urge people to do as a result of now knowing that God is at peace with us?

> We are therefore Christ's personal representatives,
> as though God were making his appeal through us. We
> implore you on Christ's behalf: Be reconciled to God.
> [2 Corinthians 5 : 20 BV]

What Paul is saying is, "Now that you know God is at peace with you, and that your sins are not being held against you, then make your peace with God."

The Prodigal Son

It's just another way of saying what the story of the Prodigal Son story was saying that we quoted in the first chapter. Here's the J.B. Phillips version of that story.

> Once there was a man who had two sons.
> The younger one said to his father, "Father, give me my share of the property that will come to me."
> So he divided up his property between the two of them.
>
> Before very long, the younger son collected all his belongings and went off to a foreign land, where he squandered his wealth in the wildest extravagance. And when he had run through all his money, a terrible famine arose in that country, and he began to feel the pinch.
>
> Then he went and hired himself out to one of the citizens of that country who sent him out into the fields to feed the pigs.
>
> He got to the point of longing to stuff himself with the food the pigs were eating and not a soul gave him anything.
>
> Then he came to his senses and cried aloud, 'Why, dozens of my father's hired men have got more food than they can eat and here I am dying of hunger! I will get up and go back to my father, and I will say to him, "Father, I have done wrong in the sight of Heaven and in your eyes.
>
> I don't deserve to be called your son any more. Please take me on as one of your hired men."'
>
> So he got up and went to his father.
> But while he was still some distance off, his father saw him and his heart went out to him, and he ran

> *and fell on his neck and kissed him.*
> *But his son said, 'Father, I have done wrong in the sight of Heaven and in your eyes. I don't deserve to be called your son any more ...'*
>
> *'Hurry!' called out his father to the servants, 'fetch the best clothes and put them on him!*
> *Put a ring on his finger and shoes on his feet, and get that calf we've fattened and kill it, and we will have a feast and a celebration!*
> *For this is my son — I thought he was dead, and he's alive again.*
> *I thought I had lost him, and he's found!'*
> *And they began to get the festivities going.*
> *[Luke 15 : 11 — 24 Phillips]*

The younger son in this story didn't know for sure how his father would receive him.
But he was so desperate, his poverty so severe, that he took the risk.

But we don't need to take such a risk.
Jesus told the story so we would know there is no risk with coming back to our Father.
And Paul has already told us that God is not holding our sins against us, so we know our heavenly Father will receive us in the same way the prodigal son's father received him.
We just need to head for home, as he did, or be at peace with God, as Paul urges us to do.

And in just the same way that the prodigal was restored to his former position as a son, so will each of us be.

Because Jesus Christ is the Saviour of the world, all of humanity will never have their sins counted against them — and Jesus is now in the process of drawing all people to himself through the work of God's Spirit.

Some are drawn early in their lifetime here, some later and many more during their future beyond planet earth.
Some of us immediately respond to our drawing, some resist a little, some resist a lot, but eventually all of us respond.

So we have a mix of God's choice in the timing of his drawing, and our choice in our response to it.
But eventually we are all restored to our original position as children of God, and, after some "cleaning up", the backstage party begins.

What About Now?

So, if this is God's plan, and it will eventually happen as God planned it, is there any advantage in being reconciled to God now, while we are still alive on this planet?

ABSOLUTELY YES !!

We would really need another book to discuss all of these benefits in detail, but for now, let's just think about this one.
So many people, including some Christians, spend much of their lives worried about the future.

> *... to be enjoying the Father's love ... is a blessing I wouldn't trade for anything ... life is wonderful not having to worry about the future.*

    What will happen when I die?
    Have I been good enough to enter heaven?
    What will happen if I haven't?
    Have I slipped up too often?
    Is there some unforgiven sin in my life?

But a person who knows that God will never hold their sins against them, no matter how many or how serious, because of what Jesus has already achieved, can stop fearing the future and get on with enjoying the present. I can assure you that life is wonderful not having to worry about the future.

And this would have been equally true for the prodigal son. If he had known that his father was not holding his sins against him, he could have returned home much earlier than he did.

He would have experienced much less discomfort and stress, and would have had more time enjoying his father's love, and his restored position, status and privileges as a son.

For me, to be enjoying the Father's love, and my position as a son, is a blessing I wouldn't trade for anything — and that will continue for all the future ages God has commissioned.

Why miss out on all that by waiting till the last moment, at the end of the ages?

So if Jesus really is the Saviour of the whole world,
    and God is not holding the sins of anyone against them,
    and everyone will be drawn to Jesus,
    and elevated to a position of a child of God,
what's all this talk I keep hearing about God's judgement?

Ahh ... it's time for Chapter Five.

CHAPTER 5

God's Merciful Judgement

IN the previous chapter, we saw that Jesus really is the Saviour of the whole world.
Some churches obviously don't believe this because their preachers frequently ask their audiences provocative questions like, "Where will you spend eternity?"
Since everyone will spend eternity with God as a result of what Jesus has done, a more useful and relevant question might be, "Where will you spend the next age?"

There is no distinction between people as far as eternity is concerned, but a huge difference as far as the remaining ages are concerned.
So let's see what judgement is and how it relates to our future.

Judgement sounds a harsh topic, especially if we consider ourselves to be tolerant, benevolent, inclusive people.
All of us make judgements about so many things every day — what

the weather is going to be like and what we should wear for the day, whether the asking price is fair or not, whether we can afford it or not, whether we should haggle or not, whether we should buy it or not.

Parents make judgements about their children's behaviour or attitude and decide on a course of action accordingly.
Students make judgements about their possible courses of study, or the subjects in those courses, and take appropriate action.

Voters make judgements about the policies offered by the various political parties, and others, contesting their local and national elections.
They also make judgements about the previous performance of the party currently in office, and the likelihood of the main opposition party doing any better, before finally deciding where to place their vote.

We make judgements almost unconsciously and then take action based on those judgements many times a day.
So let's agree that judgement is a part of life and maybe God does some judging too, both in everyday life and when the final "end of the ages" decisions have to be made.

What is Judgement?

Many people, when they hear the phrase "God's judgement" or "the judgement of God", instantly recoil as they visualise a horrendous, never-ending fiery torment in a place they call hell.
Others, who wish to paint God in a kinder light, might hope that God annihilates his enemies so that their separation from him appears more merciful.

Have you heard either of these descriptions?
I have many times.

It seems to be so common that even dictionaries, which reflect community understandings and usages of words, often define God's judgement in these ways.

Underlying such views is the misconception that judgement is the same as punishment. Actually, judgement is a decision or a verdict: not a sentence or a punishment. A judgement and its subsequent course of action are two connected, but quite separate, components of any legal system. A judgement is the result of a process for deciding between right and wrong or between guilt and innocence.

> *Judgement is a decision or a verdict: not a sentence or a punishment.*

It is this judgement which then influences what the next course of action will be.

Although our legal systems are far from perfect and open to considerable negotiation and even manipulation, they can give, at least in democratic countries, a good insight into how justice should be administered.
Let's see what happens in an ideal justice system.

'Ere Cum da Judge

A crime is committed and the alleged offender is apprehended and brought to trial.
Evidence is presented and the judge, on her own or with the help of a jury, makes her decision.

If the accused is found to be innocent, he is set free and continues life in the community.
If the accused is found to be guilty, he is taken away and given a suitable penalty for his crime, which may be a fine, or time in prison or some other rehab centre.

So a judgement may have a favourable or an unfavourable outcome, not always an unfavourable one as some people believe the word "judgement" implies.

However, in the case of an unfavourable outcome, the penalty is designed and administered with the purpose of improving the guilty person's behaviour or character so that he or she will eventually be different.
Once that penalty has been paid and the change in behaviour or character achieved, the previously guilty person will then become as free as a person who was immediately acquitted.

So whatever the initial result, judgement is a good thing, not a bad thing, as all the results of judgement immediately or eventually lead to freedom.

It is worth noting that, in an ideal justice system, the journey to the final result for the guilty is beneficial to all involved.

Firstly, guilty offenders, other than those sentenced to paying a fine, are removed from society, which frees the community from their offensive behaviour and influence.
Offenders are also prevented from getting deeper into a life of crime which may have even more serious consequences for them in the future.

Secondly, although many people might see the offender's penalty as revenge or justice so that offended members of the community are avenged for their loss and heartache, it is much more than that.
The punishment is also designed to rid the offender of his anti-social behaviour and attitudes, so that eventually he can re-enter society as a changed person and make a positive contribution to the life of the community.

Anyway, that's the theory.
That's how it's supposed to work.
That's how an ideal justice system with good judges and good laws and good administrators should work.

More importantly for our discussion here, that's exactly how God's system works.
We'll discuss this in detail as the chapter progresses.

And, as long as we don't confuse the verdict (judgement) with the consequence of the judgement process (freedom immediately or rehab leading to freedom eventually), we should have little doubt about the eventual good outcome of every one of God's judgement scenarios.

What Sort of Judgement Does God Administer?

The Righteous Judge

Many times in the Bible God is called a righteous judge.
What does that mean?
Surely a righteous judge makes good, right, fair, just, moral, ethical, transparent and justifiable decisions.

We can probably get a better feel for this by considering the opposite, the actions of an unrighteous judge, a judge who makes bad, wrong, unfair, unjust, immoral decisions.
Decisions that favour the rich over the poor, the strong over the weak, the influential over the unknown, or are biased, vindictive, vengeful or unjustifiable are examples of unrighteous decisions that spring to mind.

Thousands of years ago, Abraham was discussing God's impending judgement on the cities of Sodom and Gomorrah. You can read the full story in Genesis Chapter 18 in the Old Testament of the Bible.

He quizzed God ...

> *Will you really sweep away the righteous with the wicked?*
> *Far be it from you to do such a thing.*
> *Won't the judge of the whole earth do what is right?*
> *[Genesis 18 NIV]*

Abraham knew that a righteous, human judge would not treat the wicked and the innocent alike.
So surely God could be relied on to be even more righteous in his judgements than anything mere humankind could offer.

So what would the judgement of a righteous God look like?
If God was seeking retribution or revenge, or dishing out punishment, especially after Jesus has paid the full price for the sins of everyone, that would be unjust, unfair and immoral.

Why?
Because all people have already been forgiven — there is no price to pay.

> *Jesus Christ, the righteous one ... is the means by*
> *which our sins are forgiven, and not our sins only,*
> *but also the sins of everyone.*
> *[1 John 2 : 2 GNT]*

So the judgement of a righteous judge would have to be corrective, not retributive, and directed towards rehabilitation.
It might well involve hardship, restrictions, even pain — rehab often does.

And this applies equally to God's judgements for his "early believers" in this life as it does for not-yet-believers in the next, as we shall see a little later on.

Consequences of God's Judgement

So let's consider what the consequences of God's righteous judgements look like, what outcomes we can expect from the judgements of a loving, sovereign, righteous judge.

Justice

All judgements should be just, at the very least.
Anything less would not be fair, not right.
Justice is achieved when the punishment fits the crime.
This is what our civil laws and their penalties are meant to achieve, which is perfectly understandable since they were originally based on God's Ten Commandments given to Moses a long, long time ago.

For example, suppose I am driving on the highway and, being late for an appointment, exceed the clearly advertised speed limit and am pulled over by a police officer.
"Do you realise you're driving 25 kmh above the speed limit?"
"Sorry Sir, but I'm late for an appointment."
"That may be so, but you're breaking the law nevertheless."
The police officer remains unmoved by my explanation and issues me with a penalty notice.

> *Because all people have already been forgiven, there is no price to pay.*

It is justice that requires me to pay the prescribed penalty.
The relationship between the officer and me is an impersonal, legal one.
I am the guilty offender and he is the judge.
He makes the judgement about my actions, decides the consequence, and I comply.

Even the most ungodly of us have an inbuilt sense of justice and are quick to complain if we feel we have been treated unjustly.

If we are not exceeding the speed limit, but accused and penalised as if we were, we would be rightly outraged.
"That is unjust, not right, not fair!"
On the other hand, we don't always allow justice to motivate our own thoughts and actions, which is why the Bible calls us "sinners".

Now God is indeed a just God.
He requires us to live by his laws and has prescribed the "death" penalty for those who break them.
When we sin and break his laws, he is offended and we deserve to die — to be separated from him, to be out of fellowship with him.
That is justice, a just application of God's law.

In these circumstances, the relationship between God and us is an impersonal, legal one.
We are the guilty offenders and he is the just judge.
And that's about as far as most people get.
But there's more ... lots more. Please read on.

Mercy

When anyone voluntarily forgoes requiring a just punishment to be applied, but chooses to forgive rather than demand full restitution or payment of the prescribed penalty, that person has moved beyond being just to being merciful.

Using our driving example from above, if on exceeding the speed limit the police officer is moved by my explanation and gives me a warning rather than impose the prescribed penalty, then I would have received mercy rather than justice.
Even though I didn't deserve it, the officer would have been merciful towards me.

And the relationship between the officer and me would have become a bit more personal.

I would be having good, kind thoughts about him and even consider him a friend, and he might also be feeling good about helping someone under pressure, rather than making their situation worse.

If we met again, casually, not because I broke the law again, the meeting would be quite friendly and the way might even be open for a friendship to develop, if that was desired.

> *God, in Jesus Christ, is the Saviour of the world.*

Not many of us operate at this level.
We hold grudges, demand payment and restitution, want justice at all costs.
Although refusing to be merciful is not breaking the law, it is certainly not following the way of Christ, who showed mercy at every turn.

God is indeed a merciful God.
He does not require us to pay the penalty for our sin.
He paid the penalty for us by coming to earth as a man to die for our sins in our place.
Although we don't deserve it, the sins of everyone have been paid for — no-one has to pay for them any longer.

God, in Jesus Christ, is the Saviour of the world.
We have all been shown mercy.
And even that's not all.
There's more ... lots more. Please read on.

Grace

When justice is forgone and mercy is extended, all obstacles to a relationship between the offender and the offended have been removed.
The doorway for relationship has been opened.

But there is more!!!
What if the offended person takes the first step towards creating that relationship?
That'd be something really special and unexpected!
That would be grace in operation.

Again using our driving example, what if the officer instead of imposing a penalty (justice) and instead of issuing a warning (mercy), offered to provide a high-speed escort to my destination so that I could arrive at my appointment on time?
That would be grace in operation — overlooking the offence and giving an undeserved, unexpected favour in its place.

The offended person freely offers something above and beyond anything that can be deserved or earned or even hoped for.
Grace is undeserved favour or blessing, and, when offered to those who offend, is extremely God-like.

Les Miserables

Victor Hugo's *Les Miserables* is a well-known novel that has been performed on stage and in movies many times.
The story centres around Jean Valjean, a destitute ex-prisoner who is taken in by a kind bishop, from whom Valjean steals expensive silverware.

When apprehended, the bishop does not press charges (require justice) but instead says that he gave the silverware to Valjean (shows mercy) and then gives him his silver candlesticks as well (extends grace).
These acts of mercy and grace change Valjean's life forever.

New York Mayor

The following story is told about New York City mayor, Fiorello LaGuardia.

God's Merciful Judgement

In the middle of the Great Depression, LaGuardia went out of his way to identify with his people. It was not unusual for him to ride with the fire-fighters, go on raids with the police, or take orphans for outings.

On a bitterly cold night in January of 1935, the mayor turned up at a night court that served the poorest ward of the city. LaGuardia dismissed the judge for the evening and took over the bench himself. A tattered old woman was brought before him and charged with stealing a loaf of bread. She told the mayor that her daughter's husband had left home, her daughter was sick, and her two grandchildren were starving.

However, the shopkeeper, from whom the bread was stolen, refused to drop the charges. "It's a real bad neighbourhood, your Honour," the man told the mayor. "She's got to be punished to teach other people around here a lesson."

LaGuardia sighed. He turned to the woman and said, "I've got to punish you. The law makes no exceptions. Ten dollars or ten days in jail." But even as he pronounced sentence, the mayor was already reaching into his pocket. He took out a $10 note and tossed it into his famous hat, saying, "Here is the ten dollar fine which has now been paid; and furthermore I am going to fine everyone in this courtroom fifty cents for living in a town where a person has to steal bread so that her grandchildren can eat. Mr. Bailiff, take my hat and collect the fines and give them to the defendant."

> *The following day, New York City newspapers reported that $47.50 was given to a bewildered woman who had stolen a loaf of bread to feed her starving grandchildren. Fifty cents of that amount was contributed by the grocery store owner himself, while some seventy petty criminals, people with traffic violations, and New York City policemen, each of whom had just paid fifty cents for the privilege of doing so, gave the mayor a standing ovation.*

Here LaGuardia showed justice (required the penalty to be paid) and mercy (paid the penalty on the woman's behalf).
He then used his authority to enable grace to be shown to this poor woman.
She was guilty and therefore required to pay the fine.
She left the court without paying the fine and with more money in her pocket than she had probably ever seen.

If God's creatures can operate in this way, even occasionally, surely it is not too difficult to believe that the Creator, in whose image we are made, operates this way consistently.

God is indeed a God of grace.
God is not only just (requires a penalty for breaking his laws), and merciful (pays the penalty for us), but is gracious (invites us into an intimate relationship with him forever).
And this relationship is undeserved and free, and will include all of God's creation eventually.
How gracious is that!

So here's the difference.

◊ Justice occurs when offenders get what they deserve.
◊ Mercy occurs when offenders *don't* get what they deserve.
◊ Grace occurs when offenders get what they *don't* deserve.

God fulfils his role as Judge using all three, usually spread over a period of time.
Let's see how this might work out.

God's Legal System

God's Throne

A central feature of God's legal system is his throne.
A throne is a place from which a monarch rules.
God's throne is described in many ways in the Bible — glorious, majestic and heavenly are words commonly used.

But the writer of the letter to the Hebrews in the New Testament has another most interesting description, which we will consider here.

> "Let us then approach God's throne of grace with confidence, so that we may receive mercy and find grace to help us in our time of need."
> [Hebrews 4 : 16 NIV]

Firstly, it is described as a throne that can be approached with confidence.
Most people would approach a throne with apprehension, even fear, as the one sitting on it would have great authority and wield enormous power.
If they were at odds with the monarch in any way or approach him without due respect for the proper protocol, they would expect consequences from the throne to be swift and severe.

Justice occurs when offenders get what they deserve.

Mercy occurs when offenders don't get what they deserve.

Grace occurs when offenders get what they don't deserve.

But from this throne comes grace.
This ruler radiates grace from his throne.
Confident that grace is its character, this throne can be approached with confidence, without hesitation.

Secondly, anyone coming to this throne will obtain mercy and find grace to help them in their time of need.
I approach God's throne frequently, seeking help in my many times of need.
I never stop to think should I? Can I? Have I been here too often lately?
I am always welcome; I am always loved, accepted and understood.
It couldn't be any other way since the throne's nature is grace.

Is this the picture of the throne of Almighty God that you have been given to understand?
Most of us were raised to think of God's throne as a throne of wrath, anger, severe judgement and everlasting punishment, not a throne of grace from which the God of perfect
love rules.

But with a proper understanding in view, why would anyone be apprehensive about an audience before God's throne?
Any time — in this age or the next?

The Great White Throne

In the last chapter, we caught a glimpse of the scene at the Great White Throne.
Whether this event occurs only once at the end of the ages or is a continuing process that has already begun and will continue until the end of the ages is a matter of opinion and debate.
However, whichever view is held will not affect its purpose or result.

At the Great White Throne, all the not-yet-believers of the ages — atheists, agnostics, humanists, nominal church-goers, or whomever — are raised from their death beds and summoned to stand before the judge.

The judge appears and identifies himself.
He is the Lord Jesus Christ, the One they thought didn't exist, or was just an ancient eastern prophet, or didn't have a serious claim on their lives, or was irrelevant to their earthly lifestyle, or was a total newcomer to them.
Eyes popping, hearts throbbing, palms sweating, ghost-like faces covering minds wrestling with stark pictures of life's misdemeanours and failures.

The Lord, The Judge, The Creator ... GOD ... standing before them, with their future in his hands.
Oh My God !! (a common expression I hate, but actually fits here!)

Belief hits them as it did Thomas and Saul when they saw the risen Christ on earth.
I find it exciting to think that all who come to the Great White Throne will enter as not-yet-believers but exit as believers.

Interestingly, it might well be easier for not-yet-believers to believe at the Great White Throne than it was for not-yet-believers in the physical world during the preceding ages.
They had to believe what they could not see, whereas not-yet-believers at the Great White Throne actually see the Lord Jesus as they meet him face-to-face.

The mass conversion to belief alone makes God's judgement scene good.
But there's more!!!
They see him, they now know who he is, yet they don't really know him.

Their initial fear and apprehension is soon replaced by excitement and anticipation as they hear Jesus announce that he holds nothing against them, that their sins have been blotted out.
They stand forgiven and totally accepted before him.

So what will their response be?
We discovered this answer in Chapter Three when we quoted various Old Testament prophets like King David and Isaiah.
But here is the Apostle Paul's answer in his letter to the Philippian church in the New Testament.

> *He (Jesus) always had the nature of God, but he did not think that by force he should try to remain equal with God.*
> *Instead of this, of his own free will he gave up all he had, and took the nature of a servant. He became like a human being and appeared in human likeness.*
> *He was humble and walked the path of obedience all the way to death — his death on the cross.*
> *For this reason God raised him to the highest place above and gave him the name that is greater than any other name.*
> *And so, in honor of the name of Jesus all beings in heaven, on earth, and in the world below will fall on their knees, and all will openly proclaim that Jesus Christ is Lord, to the glory of God the Father.*
> *[Philippians 2 : 6 — 11 NIV]*

Clearly, the whole gathering will bow and worship the Lord of the Universe.

God's love, demonstrated so vividly on the cross, will eventually "compel" everyone to be reconciled to God.

And Jesus did say he would draw everyone to himself, which will not be by the compulsion of his hand or his army, but by his irresistible love and grace.

All the world's prodigals from all generations and ages will eventually want to be reconciled to the Father, and so God's plan for the universe will be achieved.
Jesus will then have completed his mission as "the Saviour of the world" and will have drawn all people to himself as he promised he would.

Isn't it interesting that this description came from a man who spent the early part of his life persecuting the followers of Jesus, clearly not bowing his knee to him?
And how did God get Paul to bow his knee?
Not with a threat: just one glimpse of the risen Saviour was all it took.
From then on Paul was acclaiming him as Lord to the glory of God the Father.
This was not a forced acclamation, but an overwhelming desire of Paul.

The Great White Throne is the place where there will also be an overwhelming desire to bow the knee and give proper recognition to the Lordship of Jesus Christ, and a major event in the completion of God's plan that we mentioned previously.
What a day of celebration that will be!

What About People Like Hitler?

Most people, including Christians, believe that Hitler should pay severely for his crimes against God and humanity.
"God's justice demands it," they say.
"Burn him in hell forever", "toss him in hell and throw away the key" and "the worst you can think of is too good for him" are commonly heard expressions.

The Christians in this group would probably change their opinion completely if they discovered that Hitler, on his death bed, repented of his sins and was reconciled to God.

Their previous stern judgement and sentence would change to rejoicing and celebration — as long as Hitler came to this point *before* he died.

> *I approach God's throne frequently ... I am always loved, accepted and understood. It couldn't be any other way since the throne's nature is grace.*

What about if he came to this point *immediately after* he died and was confronted with the same Jesus who confronted Paul on the road to Damascus? "Too late," most of them would say.

Do you think the God of love and mercy and grace would agree that one minute should make such a huge difference to a person's ultimate relationship with him?

I can't see how God's love for any of us, including Hitler, changes when our time on this planet is finished.

He is still the generous, loving Father waiting with open arms for his wayward children to return.

Where do we get such horrid pictures of a mean, vengeful God when the Bible describes a loving, forgiving and merciful Father who sent his Son to be the Saviour of the whole world?

Indeed, I can't help thinking that if God did torment Hitler forever, or annihilate him, then God would be acting the very same way Hitler had — actually even worse, since Hitler did not torture his victims forever.

And could you imagine that sort of treatment coming from the One whom Jesus said is our model of kindness and mercy?

Here's some food for thought.

Jesus told us to love our enemies and do good to them.

In this way, he said, we would be showing that we were children of God, who is kind to the ungrateful and wicked.

He then instructed his disciples to be merciful, in the same way that God is merciful.
(You can check this out by reading Luke 6 : 27 — 36 in the New Testament.)

So why then do many people expect that God will torment his enemies forever in a place they call hell, if Jesus said God is the model of kindness and mercy we are to follow?

It's hard to figure how Christians who have been forgiven their sins and been reconciled to their heavenly Father want to limit what God will do for others whose circumstances and history might be different to theirs.
He is the same God of justice, mercy and grace to those as he is to them.

Why should I even think that people like Hitler will get there in the end?
Because I have discovered that God has always been a God of compassion.
He forgives and gives people a fresh start, so often.

I know this — for three people at least.
One is me; and the other two are quite famous — King David and the Apostle Paul.
I haven't recorded my story yet, but we can read about the other two in the Bible.

King David's amazing story is described in the history books of the Old Testament, and there are additional details scattered through the Psalms he wrote.
He committed adultery with Bathsheba, the wife of Uriah, arranged for Uriah to be killed, and then married Bathsheba.

All actions have consequences — right ones have good consequences to enjoy, and wrong ones have not-so-good consequences to deal with.

So with David.
His first son with Bathsheba died very young, and his family was embroiled in scandal, rebellion and violence.

Yet, God honoured their marriage after their repentance, freely forgave them, and declared how much he loved their next son, Solomon. (You can read the story in more detail in 2 Samuel Chapters 11 and 12.)

And that's not all!
Solomon is listed in the genealogy of Jesus Christ, God's own Son, and even further, God called David a man "after his own heart".

The Apostle Paul's story is described in the book of Acts in the New Testament, and more details are disclosed in his personal letters to churches and people of the first century AD.
He was a very religious Jew and Roman citizen and became an active leader in the persecution of Christians not long after the resurrection of Jesus Christ.
In his own words, "I persecuted the followers of this Way to their death", and it was while he was on such an assignment that the risen Christ met him and his life did a complete about-turn.

God forgave Paul, gave him a fresh start, and commissioned him to take the good news about God and his love, mercy and grace to the rest of the known world.

Just to finish this part of the discussion, here's a bold thought.
Those who feel people like Hitler should never find forgiveness or be shown mercy might get a real big surprise in heaven.
Not only will they find Hitler there, saved by the same grace that saved the rest of us, but they could find that he is one of the most energetic and vociferous worshippers there.

Why should I even suggest that this might be the case?
Have a read of Luke 7 : 40 — 50 in the New Testament.

Jesus said that those who have been forgiven most will love the most.
So, how about Hitler, and the others many people think will not make it at all?
Can you imagine the sight?
Hitler in full pentecostal-style worship mode in the front row.
Wow! And why not?
He will realise he has been forgiven so much.

The Lake of Fire

So, what happens to these new believers next?
Just as "early believers" on earth in this present age have a lot of baggage to be cleaned up as they are re-formed into the likeness of Christ, restored to their original made-in-the-image-of-God condition, so do these new believers in the nearer presence of God.

In the revelation Jesus gave John (that he recorded in the last book of the New Testament) the rehab centre or correction facility was illustrated by a lake of fire.

How will this Lake of Fire do its work?
I really have no idea, but a story which has appeared on the internet over the years in various forms gives me some insight and helpful clues.
I love this story as it helps me appreciate one of God's methods of making us Christ-like, and also helps me understand the Biblical references to fire and brimstone and God's purpose in using these as cleansing agents.

> *While reading Malachi 3 (from the last book in the Old Testament), a group of women in a Bible Study were struck by the reference to God sitting as a refiner and purifier of silver.*
> *To gain a better understanding of this verse, one of the women offered to visit a silversmith,*

watch him at work, and report back to the group on her observations the following week.

She called a silversmith and made an appointment to watch him work, but didn't mention anything about the reason for her interest beyond her curiosity about the process of refining silver.

As she watched the silversmith, he held a piece of silver over the fire and let it heat up.
He explained that in refining silver, he needed to hold the silver in the middle of the fire where the flames were hottest in order to burn away all the impurities.

She asked the silversmith if it was true that he had to sit there in front of the fire the whole time the silver was being refined.
The man answered that yes, not only must he sit there holding the silver, but he also had to keep his eyes on the silver the entire time it was in the fire.
If the silver was left in the fire a moment too long, it would be injured in some way.

The woman thought about God holding us in such a hot spot sometimes, and began to see the purifying purpose in these experiences under the watchful eye of the Master Silversmith.

The woman remained silent while she let these thoughts run their course, then asked the silversmith, "How do you know when the silver is fully refined?"

> *He smiled at her and answered, "Oh, that's easy. It is fully refined when I can see my image in it."*

We were made in God's image originally, and we need to be reformed into that image for fellowship with him in eternity.
He does this in the "early believers" now through the cleansing work of his Holy Spirit, and in the later believers through his judgements at the Great White Throne and the purifying process in the Lake of Fire.

I think this story perfectly describes the purpose of the Lake of Fire. It is for purifying those who do not have life during the ages and have not had their lives changed by the purifying work of the Holy Spirit during that journey.

Different pieces of silver will obviously take different amounts of time in the flame to be purified, depending on how "impure" they were when they were placed there, but eventually the Lake of Fire will no longer be needed.

Interestingly, in the New Testament, the Lake of Fire is called the second death.
It is the death of all that offends God and that needs to be removed from those who have not had the cleansing work of the Holy Spirit involved in their lives as "early believers" on earth have had.

But when the Lake of Fire has finally finished its work it will no longer be needed and will be destroyed as Paul announced in his letter to the church at Corinth.

> *For he (Jesus) must reign until he has put all his enemies under his feet.*
> *The last enemy to be destroyed is death.*
> *[1 Corinthians 15 : 25 − 26 NIV]*

But I Have a Few Questions ?

Because of our upbringing or past church experiences, and the general views of the wider community, we might have some questions to ask after reading this chapter this far.
Most of my friends sure do.

But some of these questions will raise serious theological issues and this book is not designed to deal with these. (However, many of them are discussed on our companion website at *IBTECH Services (www.ibtechservices.com.au)* for those who wish to dig deeper. You can also ask some of your own questions on that site too.)

> *If anyone had to go to hell forever, surely it would have been Jesus, who was paying for the sin of all of us.*
> *But he didn't !*

We discussed the most frequently asked question about Hitler, and people like him, a few pages back, and we will discuss two others briefly here, trying to avoid theological terms and concepts as best we can.

Didn't Jesus Visit Hell When He died?

Yes, he did. For three days he disappeared, he was hidden, which is the correct meaning of the English word "hell".

Many Christians believe that the penalty for not becoming a follower of Jesus in their lifetime on this planet is everlasting torment in a place they call hell.
Others, who don't wish to portray their "God of love" as being so cruel, suggest that these folk will be annihilated, totally destroyed, rather than suffer the hell torture.

Even if the Bible is not known very well, let me suggest that any thinking person would struggle to reach either of these two conclusions if God is indeed one of justice, mercy and grace.

Let's begin by considering the time Jesus spent in hell (or in death, or hidden from those still on earth).
We have seen previously that Jesus paid the full penalty for the sin of the whole world.

How long was he dead? Three days.
Three days' death paid the full penalty for the sin of the world.

I now have two further questions to explore.
>   If Jesus paid for all the world's sin, how can anyone have anything more to pay?
>   Even if we could find some reason to argue that some payment is still required, how could that payment be any longer than three days?

Surely a person only has to pay for their own sin, not for the sin of others, and the maximum penalty for a person's own sin would have to be less than the 3 days Jesus paid for the sin of the whole world.

In either scenario, no payment required or a payment of less than 3 days, where is the possibility of endless torture in a place called hell for not-yet-believers?
If anyone had to go to hell forever, surely it would have been Jesus, who was paying for the sin for all of us. But he didn't!

Now let's consider what happened to Jesus after he was in hell.
He rose from the dead after those 3 days.
He came back to life, was resurrected.
Even better still, he went to heaven soon after his resurrection.

Wasn't annihilated?
Went to heaven after being in hell?

However we look at it, neither a hell of endless torment nor annihilation can logically be the penalty for sin.

Why Are Funeral Sermons Different?

What an astute observation!

I have attended more funeral services in the last few years than I have in all the previous years of my life.
It probably has something to do with having so many relatives and friends in the city where I now live who are (or were) a bit older than me.

> *If you want to hear the best sermons preached, avoid church and attend funerals conducted by Christian celebrants!!*

And I have been fascinated with the content of the funeral services.
Although these funerals have been for a mix of believers and not-yet-believers, their themes have not been that much different.

In all cases, two points have come across quite strongly.
Firstly, all those whose bodies we buried were expected to go to heaven and be re-united with their loved ones, who had likewise gone to heaven before them.
No mention of hell, or punishment, and certainly nothing about everlasting torture.

It didn't matter who the deceased was, or who was conducting the service, no-one was even considered a possibility of missing out on heavenly peace.
God's mercy and grace for all people were cited and appealed to every time.
Universal happiness was the standard, unchallenged theme.

Secondly, all were expected to have gone to heaven immediately.
They were all "in a much better place now".
No mention of going to Hades, or to hell, or waiting for a resurrection, or any other delay or stopover on the way.

Immediate, conscious transition from here to heaven was a given.

When I questioned one Christian celebrant who had led the service for a not-yet-believer about these themes in his service, he said that he didn't care "which route anyone took to get to the Post Office".

I quietly marvelled at his inference that everyone was eventually getting to the Post Office, one way or the other.
And this from a man whose personal beliefs for such non-believers include everlasting punishment in hell after waiting somewhere for a damning appearance before a "just" God at the Great White Throne.

After I wrote something similar to the above on an internet blog, a fellow blogger offered the following response …

> Thanks for sharing your thoughts on this. This happens to have been our experience exactly. We have been to three funerals in the past few months and I agree with you … funerals are the best sermons if done by evangelicals. So much hope in the resurrection and the "inescapable love of God"!!
>
> One funeral was of our dear friend's adult son who committed suicide as a professed atheist. The traditional evangelical pastor claimed him as "a beloved child of God" and recited all the classic passages on the universal love and restoration of God.
>
> Same with the Catholic funeral we attended; they read from Isaiah 25 and Rev 21. And the deceased hadn't practised Catholicism for decades!

> *The third was the same, the person had not attended the church for years but they appealed to God's grace and his mercy for all mankind and filled the service with amazing Scriptures on hope and resurrection.*
>
> *It seems so strange that mainstream christianity preaches an angry, vengeful God in the church, but hopes for and comforts grieving family and friends with something the opposite.*
> *"Jonathan from The Berean Group"*

It's quite amazing that preachers I hear being messengers of doom and gloom and eternal torment in the church pulpit have such a different message to give to those who grieve at gravesides.

It seems that the "standard" pulpit message is taught and encouraged in church circles, but a more loving, gracious, comforting message is given to grieving relatives and friends at gravesides.

So, my tongue-in-cheek advice?
If you want to hear the best sermons preached, avoid church and attend funerals conducted by Christian celebrants!!

Seriously, isn't it amazing that when real people in real-life situations are involved, the real good news that Jesus is the Saviour of the whole world is usually admitted.

So, to answer your question, "Why is this so?"
I don't really know, but my guess is that sermons for people sitting in church pews seem to be designed to keep people in line and remain faithful to the cause, while sermons at funerals are meant to comfort and give hope.

I don't find it difficult to decide which type of sermon fits the plans of the God of the Bible and sits most comfortably with the caring, compassionate, inclusive life of Jesus as he walked our earth.

God's judgement is feared by most people, even by some of those who call themselves Christians and so often announce that the God they worship and serve is a God of unconditional love.

However, the God of the Bible, is not only a God of love, but has plans for all his creation to eventually be reconciled to him and live in harmony with him forever.
So all his actions, including his judgements, are motivated by this love and are geared towards accomplishing his great purpose.

If he has written the script and created the actors in the grand stage production called LIFE, then he knows how it's all going to end.
He doesn't always force his will on us, although he has the sovereign right to do so.
But he knows how he has made us and therefore how we will respond to life's circumstances, challenges and opportunities.

And he knows that when his love, forgiveness, mercy and grace are fully revealed to us, in our time on this planet or beyond at the Great White Throne, we will respond with worship and praise.
And his rehab centre will then do whatever cleaning up is necessary for all of his creation to enjoy perfect harmony and fellowship with him in eternity.

Yes, all of us will be restored to our original made-in-the-image-of-God condition.
The good news just keeps coming, doesn't it?

Now let's wrap all this together and decide on a plan of action from here.
See you in Chapters Six and Seven.

CHAPTER 6

God - The Perfect Parent

ALTHOUGH this is a short book, we have travelled quite a long journey.
The previous chapters have considered profound topics about God, his character, his purpose and his plans. I have tried to address these topics in a way that would allow readers with little prior connection with a church or theological thought to follow my drift.

But I have used the Bible, the collection of books that mainstream Christianity generally considers is (or contains) the Word of God, to demonstrate that my story-line is consistent with the universally accepted sacred writings of the Christian religion.

So let's tie this all together using our previous parenthood theme, and then decide what to do with what we now know.

God is the Perfect Parent

From time to time throughout the preceding chapters we have looked at some of the characteristics of God by referring to the best practices of good parents here on earth.
To get a glimpse of God's character we just need to closely observe the best parents we know and discover what motivates them to parent the way they do.

Good parents really love their children, always wanting the best for them. They are motivated, even controlled, by that love, which then becomes the source for all other aspects of their approach to parenting.

Good parents are in good control of their households and their children. Although they are not smothering their children by controlling every single event in their lives, they are providing a framework and age-appropriate boundaries within which their children can make their decisions and choices.

Good parents have high hopes and aspirations for their children, are continually inspiring, teaching, supporting, encouraging, even cajoling them, to be and to do their best with the skills, talents and opportunities they have.

Good parents make huge sacrifices for their children.
The cost of parenting impacts on all aspects of parents' lives — financial, social and vocational — which they gladly pay for the privilege of seeing their children grow into mature, responsible adults.

Good parents discipline (disciple) their children.
They make judgements about their children's choices, decisions and behaviours, and applaud, reward, correct or over-ride them accordingly, with the best interests of the children governing their assessments and actions.

As good as these parents are, they are not perfect, and they will freely admit that.
Occasionally they fail and fall short of "best practice", which they regret and for which they apologise to their children, as they respond to the nudges they receive from the Perfect Parent they, consciously or unconsciously, are trying to emulate.

To get an even better picture, we could take the best aspects from each of the best parents we know and knit them together to produce the best picture of parenting that could possibly be seen on this planet.
And this picture would be pretty good, even though it comes from the parenting performance of fractured, sinful human beings.

> *The Perfect Parent will never give up on his children until they have reached their full potential.*

Although we were made in the image of God,
none of us live according to our true identity as image-bearers portraying genuine Godlikeness, even as a collective collage of our best aspects.
But with God's model before us, and the desire to emulate it, we can get better and better.

So, what do we think the picture of the Perfect Parent would look like — the One who is the Creator, who sets the standards, the One who *is* love and who will never give up on his children until they have reached the full potential he has built into them?
Let's explore that question.

God is a Loving Parent

Firstly, as we discovered in Chapter One, God really loves his offspring, all of them, including the wayward and those estranged from him, and always wants the best for them.

How could it be any other way when God *is* love?

Indeed, God's love is so overwhelming, that anyone who doesn't think so has probably not yet met him.

God's love is entirely different to the "love of God" taught in many religious circles. There are no special deals or portions for some, and lesser portions for others.
When each person's turn comes, meeting God and experiencing his love is such a consuming, even overpowering, experience.
It certainly was for Paul, who said,

> *Christ's love has moved me to such extremes. His love has the first and last word in everything we do. Our firm decision is to work from this focused center: One man died for everyone. That puts everyone in the same boat.*
> *[2 Corinthians 5 : 14 TM]*

And if anyone thinks they can avoid or reject God's love then we can safely say they haven't been exposed to it.

> *Love never gives up; and its faith, hope, and patience never fail.*
> *[1 Corinthians 13 : 7 GNT]*

Isn't it exciting to know that God loves us, each of us equally, regardless of who we are or what we might have done, and that God's love will woo us until we all fall in love with him.
The ultimate, universal romance!

God is a Sovereign Parent

Secondly, as we discovered in Chapter Two, God is in complete control of his world, which includes the human race, his special creation.
If he's not, we should not call him God, because the Bible says that ...

> *Everything comes from him;*
> *Everything happens through him;*
> *Everything ends up in him.*
> *Always glory! Always praise! Yes. Yes. Yes.*
> *[Romans 11 : 36 TM]*

John Newton was a slave-trader who became a preacher, hymn-writer and prolific letter-writer in the 18th century.
He is probably best known as the author of one of the world's most famous hymns, "Amazing Grace".
His self-composed epitaph was a powerful statement of his life transformation.

> *"Once an infidel and libertine, a servant of slaves in Africa, by rich mercy of Jesus Christ, preserved, restored, pardoned, and appointed to preach the faith he had long laboured to destroy."*

Here's a quote from him concerning the sovereignty of God.

> *"God rules all! Though he is concealed by a veil of second causes from common eyes, so that they can perceive only the means, instruments and contingencies by which he works, and therefore think he does nothing; yet, in reality, he does all, according to his Own counsel and pleasure, in the armies of heaven, and among the inhabitants of the earth."*

The last portion of this quote is clearly influenced by a statement from the Old Testament of the Bible.

> *He (God) does as he pleases with the powers of heaven and the peoples of the earth. No one can hold back his hand or say to him: "What have you done?"*
> *[Daniel 4 : 35 NIV]*

God will see done what he has decided would be done before any of us even arrived on stage.

God is an Aspirational Parent

Thirdly, as we discovered in Chapter Three, God has ambitious plans for the human race, and has always done so.
He is a God of forgiveness, grace and mercy, and has always been so. One of my favourite verses in the Bible is Acts 3 : 21.

> *Heaven must receive Jesus, the Messiah, until the time comes for God to restore everything, as he promised long ago through his holy prophets.*
> *[BV]*

GRACE — God Reconciling All Creation Eventually — was the core of God's plan right from the beginning.

It addresses both God's purpose and some elements of his timing in achieving that purpose.

It was this verse that first prompted me to hunt through the Old Testament to see how far back God had started talking about his plan to restore all things.
You might remember following the bread crumb trail of my discovery in Chapter Three.

And there are even more references than those I quoted there that show God's plan to restore all of creation has always been so — it is not a Plan B introduced as a fresh thought in the New Testament. So this idea of GRACE — God Reconciling All Creation Eventually — was the core of God's plan right from the beginning.

God is a Sacrificing Parent

Fourthly, as we discovered in Chapter Four, God has made a huge sacrifice for his creation.

The sacrifice we mentioned there was the painful and humiliating death of Jesus to pay for our sin and to give us all right-standing before God.

But Jesus sacrificed so much more than that.
Jesus is God, Creator of the universe and everything in it.

> *Christ is the visible likeness of the invisible God. He is the first-born Son, superior to all created things. For through him God created everything in heaven and on earth, the seen and the unseen things, including spiritual powers, lords, rulers, and authorities. God created the whole universe through him and for him.*
> *[Colossians 1 : 15 — 16 GNT]*

> *In the beginning the Word already existed; the Word was with God, and the Word was God. From the very beginning the Word was with God. Through him God made all things; not one thing in all creation was made without him.*
> *[John 1 : 1 — 3 GNT]*

Yet he became a man; he took on our human nature with all its limitations.

> *The Word became a human being and, full of grace and truth, lived among us. We saw his glory, the glory which he received as the Father's only Son.*
> *[John 1 : 14 GNT]*

> *Jesus Christ, who in his nature was God, did not consider equality with God something to be used to his own advantage; rather, he made himself nothing by taking the very nature of a servant, being born in the likeness of a human being.*

> *And appearing as a man, he humbled himself by becoming obedient to death — even death on a cross!*
> *[Philippians 2 : 6 — 8 BV]*

It is difficult for us to fully appreciate the extent of the sacrifice that Jesus made to share life with us here in a human body.

To help me understand something of the limitations Jesus placed on himself, I often reflect on the contrast between the normal lifestyle and abilities of a bird that soars majestically, elegantly, unrestricted and with great speed and agility in the sky with its choice to occasionally descend to *terra firma* to strut awkwardly and vulnerably on sand, asphalt and grass among much bigger and sometimes more hostile beings.

Here's a quote from Paul's teaching to a first century church which summarises the sacrifices God made to see that all of humanity were eternally safe and homeward-bound in the end.

> *Christ existed before all things, and in union with him all things have their proper place.*
> *He is the head of his body, the church; he is the source of the body's life.*
> *He is the first-born Son, who was raised from death, in order that he alone might have the first place in all things.*
> *For it was by God's own decision that the Son has in himself the full nature of God.*
>
> *Through the Son, then, God decided to bring the whole universe back to himself.*
> *God made peace through his Son's blood on the cross and so brought back to himself all things, both on earth and in heaven.*
> *At one time you were far away from God and were his enemies because of the evil things you did and thought.*
>
> *But now, by means of the physical death of his Son, God has made you his friends, in order to bring you, holy, pure, and faultless, into his presence.*
> [Colossians 1 : 17 — 22 GNT]

God is a Discipling Parent

Fifthly, as we discovered in Chapter Five, God disciplines (disciples) his offspring.

Do you remember the story in Chapter One about the six-year-old who behaved badly at his birthday party and missed out on a substantial part of the party while he was having "time-out" in his room?

While the birthday boy was away from the party, the rest of his family and friends were enjoying the celebration without him — good food, fun games and building friendships with each other, and with the adults running it.

If the behaviour of any of the visiting children got out of hand, they too might be given some time-out, but generally any lapses in the standard of behaviour desired for the party to be a success would be dealt with on the spot and, as the party continued, everyone being caught up in the spirit of the event, became more and more like the party-goers they needed to be for the party to be a perfect time for all.

The Lord also disciplines his "early believers" on the spot too.

> *The Lord disciplines those he loves, and he chastens those he accepts as his children.*
> *[Hebrews 12 : 6 BV]*

This is one of the caring and preparing tasks of the Holy Spirit residing in those who have become believers in their lifetime here, and is an ongoing process until the end of time.

Even though all of us have been restored to our original position as a result of what has been achieved by Jesus on our behalf, even "early believers" need a lot of cleaning up to be fully restored to their original "image of God" condition.

This is the training program all genuine disciples of Jesus embark upon when they are given the faith to see and believe God's love and goodness, and respond to his invitation to become his followers or disciples.

Meanwhile, back at the party ...
You might also remember that after some time, the wise and loving parent who was giving the party visited their wayward son to help him see the error of his ways and invite him to change his mindset and return to the party with a new attitude and improved behaviour.

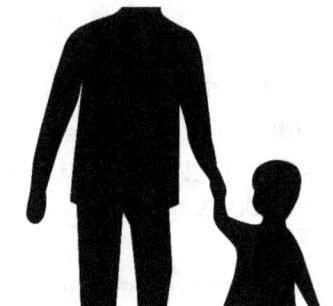

There is no question of him still being a son or of still being "invited" to the party — he would always be their son — and it was *his* party after all. Everything had been planned and done for him to enjoy his party, and would remain so.
It just needed his attitude and behaviour to be appropriate for the occasion for him to enjoy it.

Eventually, with his review and rehab completed, he returned to the party and enjoyed its continuing celebration and entertainment.

God has chosen that all of us will party together with him in eternity.

To achieve this, Jesus dealt with our sin problem so that, from God's point of view, there is nothing standing in the way to being reconciled to God and joining the party.

But to live with him, we must also be like him, returned to our original condition of clearly bearing his image, and so some correction and cleaning up is needed.

Yes, God chooses all of us — some now, some later — and the "re-conditioning" process begins.

Those whom he chooses now join the party immediately and receive his Holy Spirit to direct their on-the-spot rehab program while they're living and reigning with Christ.

Those whom God chooses later are given faith and understanding at God's throne and immediately sent for full-time rehab, fulfilling the prime function of God's seat of judgement as a throne of grace and mercy.

> Let us then approach God's throne of grace with confidence, so that we may receive mercy and find grace to help us in our time of need.
> [Hebrews 4 : 16 NIV]

After all have been restored, time ends, God becomes everything to everyone, and all are ushered into eternity.

> When everything and everyone is finally under God's rule, the Son will step down, taking his place with everyone else, showing that God's rule is absolutely comprehensive — a perfect ending!
> [1 Corinthians 15 : 28 TM]

Yes, God is the perfect parent in all ways, so will eventually bring us all into mature, responsible adulthood, ready to enjoy fellowship with him in eternity.

Some of us are more wayward than others, but the Perfect Parent's love wins and restores all humanity in the end and prepares them to live happily in harmony with him and with each other forever.

The Goodness and Kindness of God

One of the greatest obstacles people face as they explore the issues we have discussed in this book is that they don't know for sure that God is good.

We allow ourselves to think that God might do some horrid things because we are not sure he is good or kind.

As fragile and inconsistent as earthly parents are, their little children always believe the best about them, believing them to be good and looking out for their best interests.

Even when we read the Bible, and especially the Old Testament, we often fail to see the goodness of God in his actions and words.
And this is exacerbated by the common view that our life on this planet is the "be all and end all" of everything.

> *One of the greatest obstacles people face ... is that they don't know for sure that God is good.*

When we read of God removing all the world's population from the planet in Noah's flood, we see that as a terrible tragedy.
It is punishment indeed, but it is not the end by any means.
Those people are not gone, destroyed, never to be seen again.
They have just been removed from the earth.

Where are they?
They are in Hades, the realm of departed spirits, hidden from view, covered over.

And what is to happen to them after that?

Peter tells us that Jesus went to rescue them in the spirit world so that their physical world experience would not determine their ultimate fate.
Let's read about this from the Bible.

> *For Christ died for sins once and for all, a good man on behalf of sinners, in order to lead you to God. He was put to death physically, but made alive spiritually, and in his spiritual existence he went and preached to the imprisoned spirits.*

> *These were the spirits of those who had not obeyed
> God when he waited patiently during the days that
> Noah was building his boat.
> The few people in the boat — eight in all — were
> saved by the water, which was a symbol pointing to
> baptism, which now saves you.
> It is not the washing off of bodily dirt, but the
> promise made to God from a good conscience.*
>
> *It saves you through the resurrection of Jesus Christ,
> who has gone to heaven and is at the right side of
> God, ruling over all angels and heavenly authorities
> and powers.*
> [1 Peter 3 : 18 — 22 GNT]

A few paragraphs later Peter offered this explanation for the visit by Jesus in the spiritual realm to those "lost" during Noah's flood.

> *That is why the Good News was preached also to the
> dead, to those who had been judged in their physical
> existence as everyone is judged; it was preached to
> them so that in their spiritual existence they may
> live as God lives.*
> [1 Peter 4 : 6 GNT]

God really is so good, so kind.
Indeed, it is his kindness that attracts us?
Paul writing to the Christians in Rome asks ...

> *Or do you show contempt for the riches of his
> kindness, tolerance and patience?
> Don't you realise that God's kindness is leading you
> to a change of mind and purpose?*
> [Romans 2 : 4 BV]

Personally, I find it much easier to love, worship and serve the One who is kind and forgiving and has my best interests at heart than someone who is presented as angry, vengeful and looking for reasons to exclude me from his amazing heaven. Wouldn't anyone?

Let's finish this "summing up" chapter with two important, related questions.

Is God a Failure?

Although I've heard hundreds of sermons in a variety of churches and other places in my lifetime, I've never heard one entitled "God is a Failure".

Unfortunately, I have heard quite a few, and read several books, that clearly imply that God is, and will be, an absolute failure.

Whenever we notice a preacher or author make statements like ...

if you don't believe in or accept Jesus before you die, you'll burn in hell forever,
or
a person's choice of their eternal destiny takes precedence over God's choice to have everyone living in harmony with him forever,
or
the devil will have many more in his camp at the end of time than God will have in his,
or
anyone who has not had an opportunity to hear about Jesus in their lifetime will be tormented forever for not believing in him,
then we've been told by that preacher or author that God is a failure.

Hearing or reading these sorts of things prompts me to ask, "Why would anyone bother to follow, worship or serve a god as weak as this, whose plans are so easily swept aside?"

If the god portrayed by these preachers and authors is so weak and prone to failure, then he is no god at all, but a fake, a poor imitation of the loving, sovereign God of the Bible.

The God of the Bible is no failure.
His track record so far has been faultless, as demonstrated by the Old Testament prophecies which were fulfilled in events recorded in the New Testament.

So we can be sure that at the end of time, and beyond into eternity, God will have achieved all he set out to do.
He will do everything he has planned to do in his own way and in his own time.

> **The God of the Bible is no failure.**

Why would anyone call him God if he couldn't or wouldn't?

God a Sinner?

In the Greek language of the New Testament, the word for sin is "hamartia", which means to miss the mark or miss the target, or fail to reach the goal or the best possible result.

The Bible tells us that we have all sinned and fallen way short of displaying God's image in our living.

> *for all have sinned and fall short of the glory of God,*
> *[Romans 3 : 23 NIV]*

God created humankind in his image in order to reflect him and his glory on the earth. But we failed to achieve this, so we are sinners, "missers of the mark".

We probably agree on this.
I don't think anyone would say that their life has been a true, consistent reflection of God's life or that they have represented God and his government very well during their lifetime.

But do we realise that most of the world (including many Christians) believe that God is also a sinner, or at least will be?

The Bible tells us that God's plan is to reconcile all things to himself through Jesus.

> For God was pleased to have all his fullness dwell in him (Jesus), and through him to reconcile to himself all things, whether things on earth or things in heaven, by making peace through his blood, shed on the cross.
> [Colossians 1 : 19 – 20 NIV]

But most people think he will not achieve this and so will miss the mark — God will sin.

Jesus said he would draw the whole human race to himself.

> "And I, when I am lifted up from the earth, will draw all people to myself."
> [John 12 : 32 NIV]

Most people feel this will not happen and so Jesus will miss the mark — God will sin.

Paul said God is going to have mercy on us all.

> For God has made all people prisoners of disobedience, so that he might show mercy to them all. [Romans 11 : 32 GNT]

The Message version of the New Testament presents this verse like this ...

> In one way or another, God makes sure that we all experience what it means to be outside so that he can personally open the door and welcome us back in. [TM]

Most people believe God will punish the majority of humankind forever and therefore will not reach his goal, will miss the target — God will sin.

I believe what the Bible says and therefore believe God will achieve all his purposes. God is no sinner — nor ever will be.

So, What Do You Think?

Is God all-powerful, or is he not?
Is God all-loving, or is he not?
Is God's will sovereign, or is it not?
Is God's grace infinite, extending to all, or is it not?
Will God become everything to everyone, as the Bible promises, or will he not?

Let's complete this summary chapter with a quote from well-known and respected Christian scholar and author, William Barclay, who tells us what he thinks.

*"I believe implicitly in the ultimate and complete triumph of God, the time when all things shall be subject to him and when God will be everything to everyone.
(1 Corinthians 15: 24 — 28).*

For me, this has certain consequences. If one man remains outside of the love of God at the end of time, it means that one man has defeated the love of God — and that is impossible.

Further, there is only one way in which we can think of the triumph of our God.

If God was no more than a king or judge, then it would be possible to speak of his triumph, if his enemies were agonizing in hell or were totally and completely obliterated and wiped out. But God is not only king and judge, God is Father — he is indeed Father more than anything else.

No father could be happy while there were members of his family forever in agony. No father would count it a triumph to obliterate the disobedient members of his family. The only triumph a father can know is to have all of his family back home again."

[William Barclay, A Spiritual Autobiography, Pages 65 — 67]

So what is our part in all of this?
Let's explore the options in Chapter Seven.

CHAPTER 7

Our On-Stage Role

WOW, what a journey we've been on! What an extraordinary drama has unfolded before our eyes.

At the beginning of the book we called that drama "The Grand Stage Production called LIFE".
God was the playwright, Jesus the director, and we the created performers.

We have been made with a bunch of similar, common features and another bunch of very different, individual features.
Commonly, we all need food and shelter, need to be loved and appreciated, and have the ability to respond to good and bad situations with love or fear or tolerance or kindness or hostility, etc.
Individually, we look different, sound different, have different skills, talents, personalities, tastes, preferences and responses to life's circumstances.

We won't go any deeper than that — just state the obvious.

God's Specials

It might now be worth spending a few minutes thinking about where each of us is currently positioned in LIFE.
We've been born, we're alive, so we must be one of the performers somewhere on stage at this moment.

However, if you're reading this after I have left this planet, then I'm not on stage with you at this time, so let's just concentrate on your position.

A Special Person

If you've read this far you have arrived at the scene in LIFE in which you have discovered that …

>   God genuinely and unconditionally loves you,
>   Jesus has dealt with your sin,
>   God has completely forgiven you, holds nothing against you, and has opened the door for you to enjoy life in union with him forever.

That makes you a very special person — and greatly privileged.
Why? Because you have heard about God's really good news while still on stage, and only a very small percentage of God's creation have that opportunity.
And it's possible for you to start that "life in union with Christ" immediately, while still on stage, whilst most others will not get to start it until the backstage party.

A Special Gift

Now here is something really special.
If you have arrived at the scene in LIFE where you have *believed*

what you have read, even if you haven't fully understood it all, then something special has happened to you.

Really? What is that?
You have been given the gift of faith from God, the gift that allows you to *believe* that ...

> God genuinely and unconditionally loves you,
> Jesus has dealt with your sin,
> God has completely forgiven you, holds nothing against you, and has opened the door for you to enjoy life in union with him forever.

Let me explain this gift thing a bit further.
None of us makes the decision to become a believer.

We don't wake up one morning and say to ourselves, "Self, I think I'll believe in God and what he has done for me today. I think I'll believe that Jesus has dealt with my sins and shortcomings and holds nothing against me, and has opened the door to enjoy life in union with him."

It is just not a decision that we make.
Faith, the ability to believe, is given to us.
It is an undeserved gift.

Do you remember Paul, the man originally called Saul, whom Jesus met on the road to Damascus to give him instant belief?
Here's one of the ways Paul describes faith ...

> *For it is by God's grace that you have been saved through faith.*
> *It is not the result of your own efforts, but God's gift, so that no one can boast about it.*
> *[Ephesians 2 : 8 — 9 GNT]*

Saul knew many of the facts about the Christian way, but he didn't believe them.

He persecuted and harassed the "early believers", and even had them killed.
But when the risen Jesus met him and gave him the gift of faith, his name was changed to Paul and he became one of Jesus' most devoted followers and untiring co-workers.

Unfortunately, there are many good people, some even in Christian churches, who think they have to be good enough or work hard enough to earn God's kindness and forgiveness.

But forgiveness, freedom from sin, is the result of what God has done for us, not what we have done or might do for him.
Here's Paul again ...

> But those who depend on faith, not on deeds, and
> who believe in the God who declares the guilty to be
> innocent, it is this faith that God takes into account
> in order to put them right with himself.
> This is what David meant when he spoke of the
> happiness of the person whom God accepts as
> righteous, apart from anything that person does.
> [Romans 4 : 5 — 6 GNT]

Faith, the ability to believe, is God's grace gift, the result of the undeserved favour of God.
Indeed, if we claim we have done anything to assist in producing our faith, or making ourselves acceptable to God or worthy of his love and forgiveness, we are immediately discrediting God and his gracious gift and renaming it "a reward for services rendered".

Wow, I wouldn't risk telling God that his gift was just a well-deserved reward, and he owed me for it, would you?
No, rather let's do what Paul suggested to the Christians in Ephesus,

> Let us praise God for his glorious grace,
> for the free gift he gave us in his dear Son!
> [Ephesians 1 : 6 GNT]

The Next Move

So, if you are one of these special people with this special gift, what will you do next?
What are the next lines in *your* script?
Great question, but before we consider these options, let's take a closer look at the script, which we have mentioned from time to time.

The Script

We introduced the script idea in the Prologue as a way of helping us get a glimpse into the character of God and his plans for our planet. It is a very simple idea, but cannot be taken too far as God and his ways are so beyond our very limited knowledge and understanding, as you'd expect, that a simple earthly illustration would not be up to the task.

Although we were made in God's image, we are still just creatures and he the Creator, and this leaves a huge gulf between God and us, in all respects.
Nevertheless, I keep trying; I want to know as much about God and his ways as possible, and I enjoy sharing those ideas and illustrations, even if I have to keep revising them as my understanding grows.

> *So, if you are one of these special people with this special gift, what will you do next?*

But God knows my limitations and knows that I will never get to fully appreciate or understand him whilst I'm still on this planet.

However, with the glimpses of him that I do get, I know he will be satisfied with my adoration and worship and my willingness to take the part he has offered me in his stage production team.

Eternity

As mentioned in Chapter Three, one of the most challenging things for us creatures to understand, apart from God himself, is the nature of eternity, the realm where God lives.
Many people seem to think that eternity is a state in which time goes on forever, that eternal means something like everlasting.

But I think that almost the exact opposite might be true.
I consider eternity to be time-less — that there is no time at all in eternity.

Everything is in the now — everything in eternity just *is*.
Which is possibly why God said his name was "I AM" in an interesting conversation with Moses beside a bush that Moses found burning, but not being consumed.

> But Moses replied, "When I go to the Israelites and say to them, 'The God of your ancestors sent me to you,' they will ask me, 'What is his name?'
> So what can I tell them?"
>
> God said, "I am who I am. You must tell them: 'The one who is called I Am has sent me to you.'
>
> Tell the Israelites that I, the Lord, the God of their ancestors, the God of Abraham, Isaac, and Jacob, have sent you to them.
> This is my name forever; this is what all future generations are to call me."
> [Exodus 3 : 13 — 15 GNT]

Even though there is no time in eternity, God has given us time "down here" so we don't have everything happening at once.
Events happen one after the other for us in our space-time universe. Occasionally two things do happen together, simultaneously, and look at the trouble that gives us.
What would it be like if *everything* happened simultaneously?

We find this idea of timelessness difficult to comprehend, mainly because we have only ever experienced life in a world in which time is an essential and controlling ingredient.
So I have developed a few simple illustrations to help me see the difference between the eternity where God *is* and the world of time where we currently live.

Here's one of them.
A mother has a basket of goodies.

When she looks into the basket, she sees all the goodies at the same time. (Eternity)

Mother then takes items from her basket, one at a time, and gives them to her children.
The children see the goodies as they are given to them, one at a time, and in the order in which they are given. (The World of Time)

And, of course, like every good mother, she makes sure each child is given one, regardless of the child's position in the queue.

Back to The Script

Now what does this have to do with the Script for The Grand Stage Production called LIFE?
In my illustration, I see God writing the Script by looking into "mother's basket".
The Script is his description of everything that is going to happen, from start to finish — it begins with creation and ends with all creation being united and in harmony with himself.

All performers in the production have their character and role to play and their circumstances to negotiate and respond to.
Some of those events are God's to initiate and interact with; but many are ours.

We are not robots operating at the end of a long leash.
We can interpret and portray our part uniquely, as all good performers do.

Yet all the events of life, yours, mine and everyone else's, are in "mother's basket" and well known to God long before they appear on stage during the realm of time.

> **God has completely forgiven you and holds nothing against you.**

So what does God already know about your next move?
Remember, I am assuming you are this special person with God's special gift of faith.
If you haven't received this gift yet, read on anyway as you will be given it at some point.

So here's my question.
What are you going to do with the gift of faith that God has given you?
What are you going to do now that you know and believe that ...

> God genuinely and unconditionally loves you,
> Jesus has dealt with your sin,
> God has completely forgiven you, holds nothing against you, and has opened the door for you to enjoy life in union with him forever.

Well, you have quite a few options.

Firstly, you could totally ignore what you now know and what you have come to believe.
That will leave you exactly where you are, living the same life you have been living up till now.

Secondly, you could say, "That's good news. I think I'll sit on that for a while and see how I feel about it in the morning."

Thirdly, you could say, "Wowweeee, how good is that? Thank you God for doing all that for me." You could then accept God's invitation to live in union with Jesus Christ, the One who paid for your sin, and learn to follow his way of life.

If this third one is your choice, then here are some suggestions for what you might do next.

◊ Seek out a Christian church in your locality that believes and teaches what you have now discovered about God and his plans, and become involved in its life and mission. (It doesn't matter what denomination it is, nor what label is above its front door.)

◊ If you can't find a church which teaches a God of unfailing love and supreme sovereignty, and a Saviour who will be 100% successful in his mission, then try to find one that will allow you to freely believe and talk about these things and still be fully involved in its life and mission. (I belong to a church like that. Several of us believe as you now do, but some don't. However, everyone is accepted and acceptable, and we enjoy a great unity and freedom which embraces our diversity and respects people at all stages of life's faith journey.)

◊ If you don't feel brave enough to begin this search on your own, find someone you know who is also serious about being a Christ-follower and ask them to explore the local church landscape with you.

◊ If you can't find someone to accompany you, ask God to bring someone like that into your life. (I found a 'someone like that' at a local hotel — God has his people everywhere.)

◊ In your search for a church, you might bump into a house church, or a home group or a Bible study group that meets regularly in your locality, which may or may not be associated with a mainstream church. Be prepared to explore that option too.

◊ The most important thing is to become connected with other genuine followers of Jesus to help you on your journey towards Christ-likeness.

◊ If you wish, you may email *me (goodnews@ibtechservices.com.au)* and I could discuss some ideas about exploring your church landscape with you.

So Why Now?

Having read all the way through the book, you will know that everyone will be living in union with Jesus Christ eventually — at the end of the ages, at the end of the world of time.

Although we mentioned it earlier, this question might still be floating around in your mind.
"Why should I accept God's invitation to start that life right now; why not wait until the end?"
Since it is such a good question, we'll spend just a little more time on it before we finish up.

There are so many benefits of being an "early believer".
We'll note a few of them with a quote from the Bible to show that I'm not just making them up.

We are Chosen

Being a special person with a special gift says that God has selected you to live in union with Jesus much earlier than most other people — you are a chosen one, as Paul described the "early believers" who lived at Ephesus in his day.

> *Even before the world was made, God had already chosen us to be his through our union with Christ, so that we would be holy and without fault before him.*

> *Because of his love God had already decided that through Jesus Christ he would make us his children — this was his pleasure and purpose.*
>
> *Let us praise God for his glorious grace, for the free gift he gave us in his dear Son!*
> *[Ephesians 1 : 4 — 6 GNT]*

Did you notice that, as a chosen one, you now belong to God's family because God has made you one of his children?

Although we are all God's offspring, part of God's special, original creation we call the human race, the Bible reserves the title "Children of God" for his new creation, those in union with Christ, those led by God's Spirit and adopted into God's family.

From the introduction to John's Gospel ...

> *Some people accepted him and put their faith in him. So he gave them the right to be the children of God.*
>
> *They were not God's children by nature or because of any human desires.*
> *God himself was the one who made them his children.*
> *[John 1 : 12 — 13 CEV]*

And a few snippets from Paul's writings to the Christians in Rome ...

> *Only those people who are led by God's Spirit are his children.*
> *We become his children and call him our Father.*
> *God's Spirit makes us sure that we are his children.*
> *His Spirit lets us know that together with Christ we will be given what God has promised.*
>
> *All creation is eagerly waiting for God to show who his children are. [Romans 8 CEV]*

I personally am humbled by such a great privilege being offered to little, insignificant me, and I would hope you are too.

We Join Jesus in His Life's Mission

Next, we get to spend the rest of our lives here being part of God's production team on stage assisting Jesus in bringing the production to its finale, completing God's plan for the planet. (helping to hand out goodies from "mother's basket")

> God has made us what we are, and in our union with Christ Jesus he has created us for a life of good deeds, which he has already prepared for us to do.
> [Ephesians 2 : 10 GNT]

How cool is that?
God has chosen us to be "early believers" for just that purpose — to join his production team.
And, to quote a previous theme, to join his lifesaving team.

There are so many benefits of being an "early believer".

Not many beaches have only one lifesaver — there is usually a Captain and several other members of the team.
The Captain is the expert who enlists, equips and trains his assistants.
They are tested in all surf conditions, given obstacles to overcome, and awarded team membership when they qualify.

Team members share the beach patrol with their Captain and, through discipline and hard work, aim to become like him — to do as he does. They spend their time on the beach and in the water practising their skills and rescuing those who need help under the supervision of the Captain.
A good description of the role of "early believers" in the present age.

Now that sounds exciting, but it also sounds like a tough assignment, doesn't it?
Well "yes" and "yes", but we can expect that if God chooses us for this he will also equip us to make sure we are successful in it.
How does he do this?

God's Spirit Lives Within Us

Firstly, God uses and further develops the natural talents he has already built into us from birth and the additional skills and life experiences we have gained on stage so far.

But then he does something very special from there.
By his Spirit, he comes to live within us to direct, train and empower us.

> *To him who by means of his power working in us is able to do so much more than we can ever ask for, or even think of:*
> *[Ephesians 3 : 20 GNT]*

How awesome, yet that has more consequences than just getting the job done.

We Become Like Jesus

As we join Jesus in this, as we have God's Spirit living within us, we begin to become like him, become Christ-like.

Really? Have you ever noticed how sons begin to look like their fathers and daughters begin to look like their mothers as they head towards retirement age?

I have become to look so much like my father did that I get comments about it all the time.
I also notice that I have adopted some of his "odd" mannerisms too, although I don't admit it too often.

Look what the Bible says about it ...

> *I pray that Christ will make his home in your hearts through faith.*
> *I pray that you may have your roots and foundation in love, so that you, together with all God's people, may have the power to understand how broad and long, how high and deep, is Christ's love.*
> *Yes, may you come to know his love — although it can never be fully known — and so be completely filled with the very nature of God.*
> *[Ephesians 3 : 17 — 19 GNT]*

> *All of us, then, reflect the glory of the Lord with uncovered faces; and that same glory, coming from the Lord, who is the Spirit, transforms us into his likeness in an ever greater degree of glory.*
> *[2 Corinthians 3 : 18 GNT]*

> *Those whom God had already chosen he also set apart to become like his Son, so that the Son would be the first among many believers.*
> *And so those whom God set apart, he called; and those he called, he put right with himself, and he shared his glory with them.*
> *[Romans 8 : 29 — 30 GNT]*

And have you also noticed that you take on many of the habits, likes, dislikes and interests of the people you spend lots of time with? While keeping company with Jesus and working with him we start copying his lifestyle, thinking like he thinks, shooting for the same goals he does.

We all know how that works with our present friendships and with the company we keep.

The Bible often talks about the sort of "copying" changes that begin to happen in our lives as we start following Jesus.

Here's one example ...

> *You are the people of God; he loved you and chose you for his own.*
> *So then, clothe yourselves with compassion, kindness, humility, gentleness, and patience.*
> *Be tolerant with one another and forgive one another whenever any of you has a complaint against someone else. Forgive one another just as the Lord has forgiven you.*
>
> *And to all these qualities add love, which binds all things together in perfect unity.*
> *The peace that Christ gives is to guide you in the decisions you make; for it is to this peace that God has called you together in the one body.*
> *Be thankful and let Christ's message in all its richness live in your hearts.*
> *[Colossians 3 : 12 — 16 BV]*

In the words of Jesus himself, "Follow Me."

We Get To Party Big Time

We also get to start preparing for the backstage party while still on stage, as well as being one of the party organisers and "funsters" at the party itself.

> *In our union with Christ Jesus he raised us up with him to rule with him in the heavenly world.*
> *He did this to demonstrate for all time to come the extraordinary greatness of his grace in the love he showed us in Christ Jesus.*
> *[Ephesians 2 : 6 — 7 GNT]*

Pretty awesome, eh?

Aren't we so blessed and privileged to be chosen to be "early believers"?

However, that doesn't mean life becomes instantly easy and there are no battles or challenging issues ahead. Far from it.

A Friendly Warning

Indeed, there are three warnings I should give you right at the start, based on what the Bible says will happen to those who are genuine followers of Jesus Christ.

> *Everyone who wants to live a godly life in union with Christ Jesus will be persecuted;*
> *[2 Timothy 3 : 12 GNT]*

Firstly, expect some challenges from your friends who are not yet believers. These will range from genuine curiosity to teasing or even loss of friendship.

Secondly, expect some serious hostility to be tossed your way if you discuss the theme of this book in the company of some Christians.

Thirdly, expect this "Christian" hostility to be backed up by references from popular English translations of the Bible which may have been taken out of their context or badly translated from the original languages.

Here are some thoughts from Jesus on the subject of harassment and hostility.

> *Blessed are those who are persecuted because they do what God requires; the Kingdom of heaven belongs to them!*
>
> *Blessed are you when people insult you and persecute you and tell all kinds of evil lies against you because you are my followers.*

Rejoice and be glad, for a great reward is kept for you in heaven.

This is how the prophets who lived before you were persecuted.
[Matthew 5 : 10 — 12 BV]

If you wish to learn more about these warnings — the hostility and reasons for it — you can visit *IBTECH Services (www.ibtechservices.com.au)* and find the section on "Handling Hostility" there.

Although God does intervene and change our difficult circumstances from time to time, more often than not he does not. Rather, by the presence of his Spirit within us, we can approach these circumstances differently and see them as opportunities for God to do his best work.
And that's often where we see miracles happen.

I am so glad I've accepted God's invitation to start life in union with Jesus many years ago.
I'm having a ball, regardless of the challenges.
I wouldn't have missed out on any of it for anything.
How about you?

APPENDIX

The Bible and How it is Used Here

SINCE the focus of this book is The Really Good News About God, it is obvious that I will often refer to the Bible — the most extensive source of information about God, his character, his plans and the ways he uses to achieve them.

The Bible is a collection of books, rather than a single book, that were written in Hebrew, Aramaic and Greek by about 40 authors over hundreds of years. These have been translated into English (and many other languages) for us by various individuals and groups.

The translation of books which come from the ancient eastern world by translators who belong to the more recent western world is an enormous challenge and, understandably, some translators have done a better job than others.

The quality of a translation can depend on many factors — the reliability of the source documents used, the motive of the translation sponsor, the theological position of the translator(s), their qualifications and experience, etc. Some have done a better job overall; some have translated particular books better than others; some have translated very literally, others more informally.

Consequently, I have consulted many of these translations as reference sources while researching and writing this book, their influence on my understanding being dependent upon how clearly each one conveys the meaning of the texts in the original languages that concern the issue I am discussing at the time.

More often than not, I have chosen to quote from the New International Version [NIV] or the Good News Translation [GNT]. They are popular modern versions which lie somewhere between the strictly literal translations and the sincere, thoughtful interpretations or paraphrases of the Hebrew and Greek documents that comprise the Bible.

Occasionally I will use my own personal version.
This version is usually based on one of the more popular, published translations or versions, like the NIV and GNT, and then amended to represent a more literal rendering of the underlying Hebrew and Greek texts or to use 21st century English words which more clearly express the concepts being conveyed to a modern readership.
When this version is used, the quotation will be labelled as [BV] — Barry's Version.

Some of the translation issues that impact on the theme of this book are quite significant.
Most of the popular versions of the Bible, including the two I have mentioned above, are not strictly literal translations and often make confusing English translations of words that relate to the realm of time, the ages and eternity.

Indeed, if you pick up any English Bible and happen to see the word "eternity" or "eternal" or "everlasting" in its text, please take care.

Use of these English words is quite often an inaccurate translation of the underlying text leading to wrong impressions being gained, which seem to contradict the major themes of the Bible and the theme of this book.

You can find a discussion of these, and other translation inconsistencies, on the website at *IBTECH Services (www.ibtechservices.com.au)*, if you're interested.

www.ingramcontent.com/pod-product-compliance
Lightning Source LLC
Chambersburg PA
CBHW052307300426
44110CB00035B/2099